A Personal Manifesto

JO GRIMOND

A Personal Manifesto

Martin Robertson · Oxford

First published in 1983 by
Martin Robertson & Company Ltd.,
108 Cowley Road, Oxford OX4 1JF

British Library Cataloguing in Publication Data
Grimond, Jo
    A Personal Manifesto.
    1. Liberal Party
    I. Title
    324.241/0927   JN1129. L4

ISBN 0–85520–678–0

Typeset by CAMBRIAN TYPESETTERS
Aldershot, Hants
Printed and bound in Great Britain by
Billing and Sons Ltd., Worcester

Contents

Preface   *page* vii

1 The Heritage of the Post-War Years   1

REVIEWING THE SYSTEM OF GOVERNMENT

2 Local Government   35
3 Central Government and Parliamentary Reform   43

MANAGING THE ECONOMY

4 Short-Term Policies   65
5 The Long View   86

GOVERNING BRITAIN

6 Social Services: Co-operation and Community   109
7 Education   126
8 Law and Order   136

INTERNATIONAL RELATIONS

9 Foreign Policy   147
10 Defence   155

Conclusion   160
Select Bibliography   169
Index   171

Preface

Politicians should have some picture in their minds of the sort of country that they would like to live in. For my part, as I believe that all values on earth rest on individual activities and states of mind, I see the politician's task as that of building up and protecting communities in which individuals can make their own choices and develop their own personalities. It may be necessary, for the sake of others in the community, to force human beings to do, or refrain from doing, certain things: but their resulting conduct can of itself have no value.

The Alliance should be undogmatic about means but not about ends. I am all for social engineering. But to be a good engineer you must know what your engine is to be used for. You will botch the mending of a refrigerator if you think it is a washing machine.

The Alliance should be particularly careful to avoid falling into the ditches which lie on either side of the political high road. On the one hand there is the danger of elevating what are merely customary or pragmatic ways of doing things — for example, the present organization of the social services — into a species of Holy Writ; on the other hand lies the danger of producing reels of committee-made new policies.

I do not attempt to go into the details of policy-making. That is chiefly because the first task is to reach some agreement about the aims of policy. This book is intended as a contribution to the discussion of such aims. There is also, in my experience, little point in producing details of policies which can only be influential some years ahead. By then the calculations involved will be out of date.

At present the Alliance sometimes appears a little bland, even conservative. That may be what some potential 'tactical' voters want, a central party with central policies. It is not what we need. The jibe about promising 'a better yesterday', in the words of the *Economist*, should prick. I have long believed in a realignment of politics but not in that mode of British political thinking — an assembly of the centre. In the days of Lloyd George and Winston Churchill, two of its chief proponents, that meant a Tory—Liberal coalition, allowing a ministry of the best-qualified (in their own estimation) politicians to run the country. Where they were to run to was not always clear.

Coalitions have an undeservedly bad name. It is not true that England never loves them. For specific purposes — and electoral reform might be such a purpose — they can be useful. But I do not believe that a centrist group, whether supported by a new 'wet' party or by a coalition of compromise, will have much future. The voter of the floating centre should be offered not conservatism with a socialist tinge but a new radicalism. To the building of such radicalism I hope that this book makes a contribution.

Nothing on earth is wholly new. It will be seen that I have fortified my ideas by calling on what has already been written by others. The most notable of these are mentioned in the text. Even if they disagree with my conclusions, I am still most grateful to them — and to many others unmentioned. I am also indebted to Michael Hay for encouraging me to write this book, to Alan Peacock for reading the economics chapters, to Elizabeth Bland for putting the text into some shape, to Catherine Fisher for her brilliant interpretation of my handwriting and endless typing and to my daughter,.Grizelda Grimond, for general assistance.

The blemishes are my own; any truths are mostly borrowed.

Jo Grimond
March 1983

1

The Heritage of the Post-War Years

This book may be regarded as a dangerous essay in counting chickens before they are hatched. At the time of writing the result of the general election seems wide open and a hung Parliament strikes many observers as very much a possibility. In that case, would it not be more useful to explore the compromises which may have to be made rather than suggesting campaigns for which the Alliance will get no support from other parties?

I think not. The Alliance must go all out to win. For Liberals at least, to hesitate will be to throw away the great weapon now placed in their hands. For the last fifty years the Liberal Party has been tripped by the question 'Who have you got to form a government?'. Now the Alliance can offer a government of experience: the SDP is led by a man, Roy Jenkins, of proven success in government. To falter now would show a sad lack of confidence. The Alliance must convince the electorate that it is a force on its own.

Whatever the result of the general election, on the hustings the Alliance must take up its stance in the face of today's world and proclaim its hopes for the world to be. In this book I explain what I think that stance should be and how I see the future for which the Alliance should fight. It should not merely attempt to straddle the Tory paternalists and moderate Labour. It must appeal to the central body of electors but not with middle-of-the-road policies. In the short run the immediate policies of the Alliance may look like those propounded by Tories who do not believe that monetarism alone will solve our troubles. But if the Alliance is to break the mould of industry and our way of life as well as the mould of politics, it has to sketch in behind its immediate proposals what its long-term aims may be. And they must be radical, indeed risky. It has to devise some method of reconciling equality with enterprise. Under our present regime, redistribution measures aimed at achieving greater fairness in the enjoyment of wealth and opportunities too often result in bureaucratic blight and the stifling of the entrepreneur. I believe that the way to counter these is to encourage common outlooks and efforts by building on the local community, by promoting co-operation and joint enterprise among smaller groups.

Before anyone can prescribe for Britain he must diagnose her present condition. That means going back a bit into our recent history. In doing so I jump from the policies of certain Governments to a discussion of the trends that these Governments reflected and reinforced.

History is a continuous process. No doubt the causes of our present state lie far back. Perhaps we underestimate the effect of the First World War on Europe. But at least some of our present attitudes were born in, or accentuated by, the Second World War. The war saw a great increase in state activity. It also saw the growth of administrative staffs and their hangers-on. By 1944 in France the tail behind the few British units which bore the brunt of the fighting on our front stretched back through at least three Corps Headquarters, two Army Headquarters (one Canadian) and an Army Group. People compared the ease with which resources were found not only to supply munitions but also to build roads, bridges and housing in wartime with the difficulties that beset slum clearance, for instance, in times of peace. I remember myself during the 1945 Election pointing out the contrast between the 'mulberry harbours' constructed off the coast of France in the course of a few weeks with the failure, for generations, to provide islands in Orkney and Shetland with piers.

After the war faith in the power of the state persisted. Although the two most influential gurus, Keynes and Beveridge, were both Liberals devoted to individual liberty and convinced of the crucial importance of a free economy, they nevertheless believed that it was through state action that the economy could be regulated for the benefit of all and the market controlled in the interests of stability and fairness. The principles of economic and fiscal management propounded by Keynes and the welfare services proposed by Beveridge were to be under the direction of the central government.

The Labour Government of 1945 emphasized and expanded the role of the state. Its belief in centralization and state socialism was manifest in the type of nationalization which it carried through. The railways, the coal mines, the gas and electricity industries were to be great state monopolies. Direct competition, as much as capitalism, was expelled from their purview. The market and all entrepreneurial activity — though relied upon to create the wealth which, through high taxes, sustained the welfare services — were regarded with suspicion. The long-standing British tendency to esteem the professions and the Civil Service above commerce was accentuated. No attempt was made to incorporate other socialist traditions, such as co-operation, in the advance of state bureaucratic socialism. Nor was it considered feasible to submit the nationalized industries to the forces of the market or to decentralize their operations.

This growth of state (or state-supported) bureaucracies fed upon itself as more and more patronage was dispersed by those in charge of them. Further, it led to a spread of bureaucratic attitudes throughout the country and its institutions. The Tory and Liberal parties were affected. Private industry talked of economies of scale. Mergers led to the creation of huge firms which themselves aimed at a monopoly, or at least a cartel, in their fields and whose management grew increasingly bureaucratic. Those who dealt with the bureaucracies formed matching associations of their own.

As in the 1930s, some effort was made to offset the results of centralization. Special inducements were offered to industries which were prepared to provide employment in parts of Scotland, the north of England and Wales. These areas inevitably suffered from the amalgamation or nationalization of industries whose headquarters settled in London. The concentration of power in London made the capital a magnet particularly for top people, whether in politics, industry, public service or the professions. The efforts to attract industries to the depressed areas were themselves conceived and administered in London. No attempt was made to allow autonomous powers to be exercised in Scotland, Wales or the provinces of England. Here we see another feature of the thinking which was dominant in the 1920s and 1930s, was accentuated by both wars and reached its peak under the Labour Government of 1945—51.

First, there was the failure to remove the causes of the trouble. Admittedly, no one could arrest the decline of the heavy industries, but the blood of Britain outside the south-east of England was being drained away by bureaucratic centralization. Instead of decentralizing power, attempts were made to offset the results of centralization while pursuing the policy. And the very efforts to revitalize with the left hand what was being strangled by the right were themselves directed from the centre. The grants and subsidies offered to industry increased its dependence on London. At the same time the implementation of most of Beveridge's proposals was uniformally administered from the centre. The same measures were to apply from Shetland to Cornwall. The welfare services, of course, increased the dependence of individuals on the state, as the grants and subsidies increased the dependence of industry. Incentives to work, or to work efficiently, were reduced. Everyone was taught that the state (that is, their fellow taxpayers) owed them a living. The results were predictable.

I am not here concerned to argue the case for or against this development, still less to apportion praise or blame. In my book *The Common Welfare** I have considered some of the results. One of the most striking has been that although the standard of living of the poor may have been raised and the gap between the standards of life of the comparatively poor and the comparatively rich has narrowed, the rift between rich and poor communities persists. The communities of the old industrial areas in Scotland and Wales, Northern Ireland and the north of England remain worse off, by almost every test, than those in the south and south-east of England. In these latter regions the prospects of the poor with respect to education, health, housing and work are better than those with larger incomes in many communities on the Tyne, Clyde and Mersey or in Belfast. I argued in *The Common Welfare*

* London: Temple Smith, 1978.

that we need to put more stress on improving communities. Events in Brixton and Liverpool since that book was published support my contention. I hope the Alliance will take the same view. If it does, it will have to tackle the distribution of power in a more radical way than has hitherto been attempted and to flout some established theories.

If this change is to be effected, we must accept that the centralized thinking behind the measures of 1945−51 achieved some good results. The welfare services have improved the lot of the population. All have benefited. It is not now necessary to argue about the past but to consider the future. Further, the arguments for a centralized system are serious and must be admitted. One of the more important of these is that any increase in prosperity entails the redistribution of wealth, power and prospects. The providers must be the richer taxpayers, the more powerful institutions. If indigent cities and communities are to be helped, we must discriminate in their favour. This must be a national decision. Another argument is that the same standards (for example, in education and health) should apply everywhere; no child should be offered lower standards in essential services just because he or she happens to have been born in a remote country area or a city slum. A third argument in favour of centralized control is that the management of the economy must remain with the central Exchequer. Fourth, the performance of some local authorities prompts careful consideration of the merits of decentralization. Under some authorities the citizens must be thankful that there is some bridle upon their representatives and nervous that any more power will be entrusted to them. Many local authorities preside over sharply divided communities in which a majority is found permanently from one party. The notion that in such communities there is any binding sense of unity, any disposition to accommodate the views of the minorities or any chance of democratic change of government such as exists at Westminster is a myth.

These arguments will be considered at greater length in later chapters. Here I want to say only that they raise valid points which must be borne in mind. Some areas of the country will need extra assistance. However, the need for standards to be high does not mean that they must be uniform, nor attained by identical methods. Good education and good health can be promoted by different means in different places. Nor, as I have said, has the attempted imposition of the same regulations in, say, Sunderland and Bournemouth meant that the citizens of these towns share identical advantages. For the management of the country the obligations and powers of local authorities must be more closely defined. In order that local government and services may be regarded as satisfactory, more attention must be given to community boundaries and more thought to how the services should be administered.

The decentralization of government and services will be resisted by the present bureaucracies and by the trade unions, which under the influence of the British climate are themselves centralized and accustomed to central regulation. Many members of the SDP rose to high office under the present system. Messrs Owen and Rodgers and Mrs Williams in their books* and Roy Jenkins in his speeches have come round to favouring smaller units and a greater distribution of power, but it would be folly to attempt to change what has been the prevailing habit of mind too suddenly and without a considerable campaign to explain to the public the issues at stake.

The confidence in our national institutions displayed by the 1945 and 1950 Labour Governments, sustained by Gaitskell and his followers (and, indeed, by Tories and Liberals up to Suez), ran into trouble on two fronts. Both Labour's plans for the management of a mixed economy in which the Government interfered to a greater and greater extent and the extention of the nationalized monopolies depended upon the co-operation of sympathetic leaders in the trade unions — leaders who did not use their industrial strength for political ends even if they approved of a wide measure of state socialism, did not look forward to the indefinite extension of the state and were moderate and co-operative in their demands. But the generations of the Bevins, the Deakins and the Feathers were succeeded by a much more abrasive clutch of left-wing union leaders, who were prepared to use the power which nationalized

---

* David Owen, *Face the Future*, London: Jonathan Cape, 1981; William Rodgers, *The Politics of Change*, London: Secker and Warburg, 1982; Shirley Williams, *Politics is for People*, London: Penguin, 1981.

monopolies gave them to consolidate and extend their own position at the expense of the general good. At the same time the general good was also threatened by the huge entrenched bureaucracies which became interests on their own. No longer was the Civil Service a fairly small segment imbued with a sense of its duty to the public and acting in the public interest either as administrator in the traditional non-commercial fields of defence, civil order and broad economic policy or as arbitrator when sectional interests clashed. Now it was an economic interest on its own, pursuing its own ends.

Indeed, the public service had developed into a series of interests. As is evident from many books about British government and from the reminiscences of politicians and bureaucrats, 'government' has expanded to become a huge agglomeration of bureaucracies, all pursuing their own interests. The House of Commons now has many committees anxious to extend their powers. The spending departments of the central government all clamour for more money, as do the boards of the nationalized industries and innumerable quangos. For some purposes the Cabinet must be regarded not as a central power house but as a battlefield on which departments fight for more resources. It has been known from time out of mind that people are more careful with their own money than with that of other people, that organizations tend to grow in size and to demand more powers: Parkinson's Law has never been refuted. The Prime Minister's office and the Treasury sometimes seem like the bastions of a medieval monarch trying to keep feudal barons in some sort of order. Barons will fiercely resist retirement (are not the Commissioners of the Great Exhibition still with us?) and, just as fiercely, the dissolution of their fiefs. The habits of bureaucracies are as old as human history. Rome, the Spanish Empire, Versailles, Moscow, all tell the same familiar story. In our day it is only recently that the power of various organs of the state (the Bank of England, for example) has begun to be probed — as in *The Power Game* by Jock Bruce-Gardyne and Nigel Lawson.*

Apart from the proliferation of bureaucratic attitudes and their present strength, we have had to contend with the decay of any

* London: Macmillan, 1976.

widely held morality — indeed, any morality at all — or any accepted fabric of life. More and more are we described as 'civil servants', 'businessmen', 'unemployed' or 'members of one-parent families'. We are expected to act out our roles, join appropriate organizations and surrender our freedom of choice to those organizations, which are not bound by allegiance to a common good or even a class interest. The aim of each is to pursue its own interests — that is, the interests of those who run it. With the emergence of this attitude towards the individual, who is no longer looked on primarily as a person of all-round capabilities, as first, and before any other trait, a human being, has gone a decline in deference, awe, respect. Destructive as this has become, at first it led to a welcome curiosity, a desire to take part. The demands of students to be treated as full and active members of their universities was surely a good thing.

Much has been made of the rupture with accepted conventions and morality in the 'swinging sixties'. Adultery, divorce, drugs and thuggery are blamed upon the repudiation of personal or family responsibility and therefore of the punishments and sanctions which formerly fell on those who broke the code of morality or, in some cases, the law. It is sometimes forgotten that the disruption and violence attributed to the throwing away of old restraints was exaggerated by the attention paid to it by television, the newspapers and sociologists. In their first careless rapture the sixties at their best tried to promote a new vision of morality, not entirely divorced from personal responsibility. Love, enjoyment, mutual good will were to take the place of repression. It was indeed a repetition of an old story. Every revolution starts with dancing in the streets; then violence and the guillotine take over. Socialism believed that, given a chance, the brotherhood of man and devotion to the common cause, the Christian values, would replace greed. At first these motives were openly proclaimed. Perhaps socialism would succeed if they could flower. But the development of bureaucratic attitudes, the centralized state so vastly accelerated by the legacy of 1945, smothered the essential but discredited motives of idealistic socialism.

The hopes of the Gaitskellite socialists were dashed. The nationalized industries proved to be neither happy nor efficient.

One powerful argument for state activity appeared to be that it would engender new motives. No longer would managers seek only to maximize profit and their own emoluments; they would be moved by a desire to serve their country and the common good. No longer would workers feel liable to exploitation by private greed; they too would gladly give of their best, knowing that the fruit of their labour would not fill the pockets of shareholders but would increase the common good and improve the lot of their brother wage-earners. Yet from the first there was some confusion about the nature of the nationalized industries, and it was apparent that altruism was not to be their driving force. Those who worked in them proved to be just as keen to look after their own interests as any employee of capitalism. But these industries bestowed two great advantages on their employees. First, they were for the most part monopolies and hence free from competition; second, the taxpayer stood behind them to supply unprofitable investment and to make up the continual losses. And nationalization did not solve the problem of surplus value. The workers, who in any case did not pay much attention to the doctrine that they were robbed of the surplus they created, were no more pleased to be robbed by the state than by a private employer. Nor were they wrong, for the state turned surplus value to no better purpose, and frequently to worse, than the capitalist.

It was suggested too that by seizing the commanding heights of the economy the Government would be able to regulate the economy more efficiently in the public interest. This theory proved almost the opposite of the truth. The enormous growth of the public sector made the economy unmanageable. The fixing of wage and salary rates became more and more difficult. The nationalized industries swallowed a large proportion of the resources available for investment and put them to worse use than the private sector would have. The industries chosen for nationalization were largely those which were obsolescent or at least required only on a diminishing scale. They were not the heights but the quagmires of the economy, requiring endless subventions to keep them going. By taking responsibility for them, the Government saddled itself with a heavy handicap in managing the economy. As their nominal owner, the public was milked again and again for their benefit. Had the Government been able to stand back and deal even-handedly with the whole economy, its task would have been much easier. Like the foster-parents of cuckoos, the private sector had to work harder and harder to feed the state monster.

The nationalizers never faced the difficulty that Parliament was not elected or equipped to run — or even to supervise the running — of industry. This soon became apparent. But what was then to be done with these industries? The myth persisted that if managed as commercial enterprises, though without the character-istics of such undertakings, they could live by themselves. So together with the Post Office, they were shipped off into a world of their own, free from parliamentary questioning or the constraints of the market. I once asked a Conservative Minister of Transport what he proposed to do about losses on the railways. He replied that railways had been ordered by statute to make ends meet and that was that. Not even King Canute's courtiers at their most absurd ever said anything as stupid.

At the same time the prospect of perpetual growth became obscured. Indeed, state socialism was a prime factor in the produc-tion of the clouds that overshadowed it. Therefore there was no steady increase in wealth from which a high rate of tax could be extracted for the social services, the demands of which by then far exceeded the estimates made by Beveridge. The belief that efficiency could continuously be improved by forming bigger and bigger units turned out to be an illusion.

Here we meet what is perhaps the central fallacy of state socialism. The bureaucracies that it spawns try constantly to extend their empires and their emoluments. It is in the nature of government to grow. At the same time these bureaucracies depend entirely upon being able to live off an expanding non-state economy. But the nature of state government makes it certain that the private production sector will contract as the state expands.

But 1945 and its aftermath — indeed, the trend since the beginning of the century — had left such powerful vested interests behind that no effort was made to meet the growing difficulties into which we were running. These vested interests were to be found not only in the bureaucracies and in big business but also, and still more, among intellectuals. The academic and public relations worlds, the press and politics, all were deeply imbued with statism. This was as true of the Conservative and Liberal parties as of the Labour Party — hence the phrase 'Butskellism'.

Increasingly bereft of social cohesion, uncertain about the validity not only of traditional morality but of any morality, the British pinned their faith to material progress. When this faltered many of them, particularly some immigrants, already uprooted, sensed around them a desert across which appeared the marvellous Never-Never-Land of the TV advertisements — a land that the advertisements implied was theirs by right. In this process the welfare services became entangled and distorted. On the one hand, they were more than ever necessary, and more people came to depend upon them; on the other, they themselves became bureaucratic. Their interest lay in perpetuating, not curing, this dependency. Education was contaminated. The high hope that an educated democracy would look to the long term and the general good, would rate the quality of life above the quantity of distractions, was not realized. The health service discovered that as the nation's health improved, so demand grew, stimulated by the service itself, now increasingly influenced by its growing army of administrators.

Significantly, British art, which had largely escaped the bureaucratic embrace, flourished. More people painted, sang, acted than ever before. The reputation of British painters, musicians, dancers and actors stood high in the world. So far the art schools had been allowed to go their own way. Substantial public money was granted, but the dead hand of central organization and bureaucratic conformity had not withered individual talent.

The spread of bureaucratic blight and the disintegration of the British political structure was accentuated by the local government reform of 1972. As with any so-called 'reform' of the period, this led to a further growth of vested interests and of bureaucrats. The functions and finance of local government were inadequately considered. As a result, local authorities have now spread into every kind of activity; new sets of vested interests standing in the way of change or efficiency have grown up; and rates have rocketed, driving employment away. The local government explosion has been strangely ignored by political theorists, but it is one of the most serious developments to have taken place in post-war Britain.

The press, radio and television have played their part in casting the mould that has confined us since 1945. It is a part which deserves a balanced judgement. Like most inventions from alcohol to the motor car, the value of the radio, press and television depends on how they are used. In some ways they have been used well. They have preserved freedom of comment. They have been blamed for some of their virtues (for example, their refusal to obey governments) and blamed also for many vices which are those of their clients. They have invigorated politics. Indeed, without its coverage by the TV, the press and the radio, politics would have been totally deflated. The best commentators have spread a knowledge of current affairs unknown in previous generations. History, art, literature have come to life over the air. By the magic of the set millions of people have been induced to watch plays and to follow stories which otherwise they would have shunned.

We should not exaggerate the power of the press and broadcasting. Gladstone alone had more impact on people, even those who had never seen him, than all the TV stars put together. It is significant that those who read the news off a tele-prompter or the weather off a chart are the heroes of the TV screen. The radio and the TV set supply an opium much appreciated by the British. A TV news-reader or some of the most popular interviewers can be relied upon to stick to their tele-prompt. Nothing to provoke thought need be feared.

This was far from true of such examiners as Ludovic Kennedy, Robin Day, Robert Kee or Alastair Burnet. Nevertheless, the negative power of TV, etc., was considerable. And to be kept off the air was damaging. Confined at first to the BBC and then to the BBC and ITV, radio and television were inevitably ingrown. They too were run by bureaucracies. Their controllers, commentators and those who selected news items came largely from the same London, liberal, middle-class background. The same political pundits appeared on programme after programme, year after year. That most of them were very good did not prevent a certain attitude from developing that was inimical to new thought and unwilling to accept that much of importance could be happening away from their metropolitan haunts. They contributed to the centralized outlook. The academics who appeared readily were political tipsters rather than political philosophers. Politicians were invited to broadcast because of their eccentricity, the silliness or abrasiveness of their latest remarks. Like the dinner bell to Pavlov's dogs, certain names made news editors and programme constructors prick up their ears. Such names enjoyed exposure whether their owners said the earth was flat or round. And the reputation they acquired for wisdom on the air gave them prominence in the House of Commons.

As for the press, much of its coverage of politics was devoted to gossip or sensation. Political journalists were determined to find dissension everywhere. Their staple was the disagreements that they constantly claimed to find within the political parties. Even when their disagreements were trifling, they hogged the headlines. Except in the leading articles of the more expensive papers, discussion of issues was not wide or deep. Advertising, particularly that on TV, encouraged dreams and avarice, as I have said. Like broadcasting, the papers gave great pleasure, which was a boon to be cherished: they hardly encouraged the British people either to participate in the running of their own affairs or to develop a sense of community which, when necessary, would stimulate unselfishness — and they did their bit in promoting sensation and violence.

The Suez fiasco could have had its benefits. It could have been seized upon as the occasion for shaking the British out of their complacency and tackling some of the defects of their economy. For a moment the British people saw the true state of their affairs at home and their position in the world. In that moment of truth they perceived that so far from being the brilliant Greeks of the world, their Government was a set of bunglers who had not even the confidence to go through with their bungle and that in the world outside we were dependent on the good will of the Americans. But, having outsmarted Mr Butler by a rapid transformation from arch Suez hawk to mildest of the doves, Mr Macmillan went about assuring everyone that all was well and that the British were the best people in the best of all possible worlds. I myself heard him at some Anglo-American function make a speech of breath-taking complacency about our special relationship with the USA, which had recently rapped us contemptuously over the knuckles. Had Butler, a man of greater insight and weight, become Prime Minister, he might have traded on the willingness of the nation to face reforms and carried out some much needed structural changes in, for instance, industrial relations with a fair degree of assent. Under Derek Heathcote Amory the balance of trade, inflation and our economic position in the world were as good as they were ever to be again. But the opportunity to make good the flaws in our way of doing things and to revise our mental attitudes was missed; instead we were administered renewed dollops of soothing syrup. Further, politicians were encouraged to sustain the illusion by which they persuaded each other, the press and, through the press, the public that by making a speech they had actually achieved something. This state was to reach its apogee in Harold Wilson's phrase about the 'white heat of the techno-logical revolution'. The British, finding no effective inducement to enter the furnace, kept out of the way of any such heat. The nationalized industries, the government bureaucracy and its counterpart in large-scale private industry, now more and more dependent on government grants, went on as before.

In fact, from Suez onwards we began to show all the classic signs of a country in decline. We sustained a vast top-hamper of government hangers-on, reminiscent of Versailles. The way to power and affluence was not to assume personal responsibility for one's own life and to foster initiative but to become a courtier of one of the various bureaucracies. The upper or richer classes were more than ever convinced by their education and upbringing that the road to affluence and prestige, to the indexed pension and the GCMG, led through the professions and the Civil Service. The working class was to a great extent organized by trade unions, which cared nothing for the efficiency of industry — indeed, conceived that it was their duty to frustrate attempts to increase profitability — and wasted endless time on disputes even when not on strike. The Treasury became more and more out of touch with industry as it struggled in the north of England, Scotland, Wales and Northern Ireland. Furthermore, it seemed to regard small-scale private business as essentially a means of tax evasion to be tied up in a web of restrictions, regulations and requests for information. The tax system itself grew complicated to the point of incomprehensibility. The effort of Mr Wilson's Government to create a Ministry of Economic Affairs may have been misguided in detail; it was probably right in intention. It was killed by the Treasury, which it threatened.

From 1974 inflation and unemployment steadily increased both under Conservative and Labour Governments. 'Stagflation' confounded the macro-economists.

Our troubles were political. They arose out of the organization of our industries, our industrial relations, our attitudes and the structure of our politics. All the paraphernalia of the economists' supply and demand, the Phillips curve and so on were turned into junk. The presuppositions of economics (that higher prices would control demand, for example) were frustrated. Higher prices merely led to demands for higher wages. Over the whole public sector the carrots and sticks which were supposed to regulate our behaviour had no effect. Even in the private sector the welfare services, government grants and subsidies distorted the operation not only of classical economic theory but of any economic theory at all. (In parenthesis I might say that I have always been sceptical of any simple analysis of motives. Some people like routine work; others take responsibility. Many people would much rather work than be idle. They would still work even if they were offered more on the dole.)

So we arrived at the General Election of 1979. In considering the era which went before — right back to the war — we should remember that the British people were probably better off then than ever before. Nor was Britain without talent and stimulation. Intellectual and artistic talent are not necessarily the products of a successful political or economic society. Two of the most extraordinary flowerings in all history took place in Edinburgh between, say, 1770 and 1830 and in Vienna between about 1860 and 1925. Yet the politics of these cities at the time of their glory were, by our democratic standards, deplorable. Deplorable too, according to our lights, were their housing, the living conditions of their poor and the efficiency of their bureaucracies or courts of justice. Indeed, the centres of the Renaissance in Italy would have earned no marks at all from those who set themselves up today as judges of good order and good government.

Though to my mind the methods of state intervention have been mistaken and the degree to which the socialist establishment thought that it could run the country has been over-estimated — with sad consequences not only for economic planning but also for the physical planning of our cities — yet we should not swing to the other extreme and damn all state operations. What is needed is a reconsideration of the role of the state.

The Tory and Labour parties of the 1960s and 1970s were stuck in a cutting from which they could not escape. The Labour Party was bound to the trade unions, its only source of money. Without the funds which the unions supplied, the Party would have been bankrupt. The trade unions were deeply conservative in their addiction to state socialism, which they saw as the guarantee of their own power. The taxpayer made an admirable employer, from their point of view, as he could be squeezed to make good the losses caused by over-manning, inefficiency and the survival of obsolete practices. The union leaders had no interest in making Britain richer or more competitive. Within the Labour Party too there was no new thought. Its policy was to reinforce failure. If planning, housing, the health service and the public sector were in trouble, its solution was to spend more money on them and to extend state intervention on the current model. The burden of rising central and local government expenditure and the quangos was, the Labour Party thought, to be financed out of an expanding economy. But the economy did not expand. Nor was it apparent how such nostrums as the nationalization of the banks or the abolition of the House of Lords — policies beloved of the left — were to create expansion. As Britain, dependent upon world trade, was apt to suffer if her inflation or her inefficiency led to either an increase in imports or a flight of capital, tariffs and restrictions were to be imposed. In fact, the siege economy and further infringements of freedom were about the only remedies recommended by the increasing influential Labour left.

The Tories and the right of the Labour Party still put their faith in manipulating the macro-economy by means of central fiscal and financial policies. These looked more and more ineffectual.

Increases in the money supply and government spending resulted in no great rise in employment. As the 1974—9 Labour Government eventually admitted, higher inflation did not reduce unemployment. As for the Tories, their efforts to reduce non-productive public employment made little progress. Indeed, the so-called reform of local government led to a massive increase in the number of bureaucrats and to an extension of interference with the individual by the public authorities. Until 1980 the Tories made no effort to denationalize the nationalized industries. Indeed, some extension of nationalization took place under the Tory Government. The Tories, like the Labour Party, had to assure their backers (big business and the City) that nothing drastic would be done. As I have said, big business itself was becoming more and more bureaucratized. Its managers were not entrepreneurs. They usually looked to their salaries, perks and pensions for reward rather than to distributed profits in which they often had little interest.

If success is to be measured by invisible earnings and the rewards of those who work in it, the City of London has been highly successful — so successful in fact, or so adept at giving the impression of success, that it has evaded nearly all suggestion of change, let alone any practical steps to change it. Nevertheless, the City has contributed to some of the features of post-war Britain which are much in need of change. It has done little to assist British industry. Its help for small and new businesses has been ineffectual. In spite of the Macmillan and other reports, it has not been easy for small companies to get capital. One of the instruments of the banks, Equity Capital for Industry, was conspicuously unsuccessful, though the Industrial and Commercial Finance Corporation (ICFC) was a success. One of the handicaps from which the industrial areas and the regions far from London have suffered is the drawing off of their savings into government securities, building societies, pension funds and the like. The dearth of capital, partially the product of the policies of the central government, have had to be made good (a typical piece of British administration) by central government itself. Taxes have been collected by a large and expensive machine and paid back to those fleeced. The City meanwhile has created trusts and pension funds and, in the early 1970s, financed a property boom. The investment trusts, standing always at a discount, have been unadventurous, their management complacent and their investors, in times of inflation, badly served. Like that of other directorates in too much of British finance and commerce, their main purpose has seemed too often to be to guarantee safe jobs with slowly increasing salaries for their directors. Moreover, trusts and pension funds have absorbed a growing proportion of our savings.

The Tory Government of 1979 came into office with the intention of reversing the trend to socialism in all its forms. But the Tory Party in the Commons and in the Government naturally contained many of those responsible for their party's policies of the previous thirty years, which had been tolerant of the socialist advance — indeed, had contributed to it — and had implicitly, if not explicitly, accepted the 'ratchet effect'. Changing into reverse gear would anyway have been difficult. The plan was further hampered by the acceptance of the Clegg recommendations for public service pay, the increase in VAT and the policy of making energy as expensive as possible. This last was another example of the disposition of the Treasury, and perhaps of the Bank of England, to look at the manipulation of money rather than at the actualities of the world. The increase in the price of oil allowed the balance of trade to look good, increasing the value of the pound at the expense of the exporting industries. The steep increases in the prices of gas and electricity were treated as a form of taxation used to further the Chancellor's fiscal and financial aims. As a result, industry gained little directly from North Sea oil and gas, indirectly suffered some disadvantages and was faced with higher energy costs than its main competitors. Had such a policy been pursued over coal in the nineteenth century, the industrial revolution in Britain would have been aborted.

Since 1980 the Government has been more effective in resisting wage and salary claims in the public services. But its policy has serious defects. It has failed to persuade the people at the top to set an example. It may be true that the Crown, the judges, the top civil servants and others have been deprived of the full value of awards made to them by the Top Salaries Review Body, but that body is itself a product of the time when it was assumed that we could all chase our tails over inflation. Further, the Crown and the top people generally, with their perks and indexed subsidies and pensions over and above their salaries, are well sheltered. In any case, both an example and a narrowing of differentials are very necessary. In the balance sheets of less profitable public companies it is noticeable that while shareholders get less or nothing and wage-earners are laid off, the directors steadily increase their emoluments and are never sacked except with a golden hand-shake. The method of granting increases by a percentage of existing salary and wage rates favours the higher-paid.

The Government has tried to act on the money supply rather by making money expensive than by limiting the amount available. Interest rates are high, but there has been little control of the credit base. It is convenient for many activities of the City of London to have money readily available even if it is expensive, but once again this is a policy which bears hard on productive industry.

In its effort to reduce the public sector of industry, the Government has sold off the more profitable bits of the nationalized industries. Little effort has been made to assist the formation of co-operatives among the workers to take over at least parts of certain industries — for instance, the catering on the railways. The management take-over of the road services was the most promising of its transactions. For if the alternative to nationalization is ownership by pension funds or trusts, remote from the activities of the firms concerned, or even by dwindling band of private investors, we shall see no improvement in industrial relations and provide no incentive for greater efficiency. If and when a Labour Government regains office, we shall have neither demonstrated that there is an alternative to nationalization, which will give more people a stake in industry, nor enlisted the interests of the workers. The obvious way to improve efficiency, reduce friction in industry and promote a common effort is to involve workers more directly in the success of their enterprises.

Meanwhile, British industry has, to adopt the euphemism of the Government, been 'slimmed'. It is no doubt fitter. It is certainly a lot leaner. Some firms will never return; in others, for a time at least, both management and men will have learned the lesson that over-manning and inefficiency cannot forever be offset by subsidies and inflated prices, and that wage and salary rises cannot be maintained if productivity and profits fall. But little has been done to alter the structure of industry, and some of the old habits will revive. As for reductions in the public service, some quangos have been abolished and some staffs reduced. The Civil Service, which was 732,300 strong in 1979, now numbers 666,400, but the amount of legislation has actually risen. There have been four local government Bills applicable to England and Wales and three to Scotland. They lay more duties on the local authorities, whose staffs have already swollen so enormously.

After four years in office the Tories leave the country in a parlous state. Real national income has fallen by at least 6 per cent. Manufacturing output is down by one-fifth. Unemployment is over 3 million. The only concrete benefit to which they can point is a reduction in inflation — but to a level which will probably rise.

The Tory Government's mistakes of commission have been serious. Sir Geoffrey Howe's first Budget boosted inflation. The Government has relied far too heavily on high interest rates as a means of economic control and has done too little to reduce the monetary base. It has held up the cost of energy when a reduction would greatly have benefited industry of all kinds. But its sins of omission are worse. It has refused to undertake even productive investment in the public sector on a scale adequate to take up some unused resources. It has held down demand when some increase would not only have stimulated current employment but also enabled industries viable in a longer perspective to survive. Most serious of all has been its failure to introduce economic or political structural reform.

Belatedly it has indeed sold off some nationalized undertakings and introduced some risk capital into the nationalized industries. But it is almost thirty years since Arthur Holt, then a Liberal MP, and I suggested that some of these industries should raise capital in the market. Deflation has been achieved largely at the expense of the private productive sector of the economy. Even when nationalized industries have been hived off (Telecom is an example), they remain near-monopolies. Competition has not been let off the leash. Under the Tories the percentage of output taken by the Government has actually risen — it now stands at £57 in every £100. The Government has done little or nothing to improve industrial relations. The one management take-over it has allowed has proved a success, but this example has not been followed in its dealings with other parts of the nationalized sector. If trade revives, the old troubles of our economy will revive with it. The tax system has been made even more complicated, so that the incentives offered to small businesses have been largely nullified.

As for political reform, apart from the development of the special committees in the House of Commons there has been none. Yet it is obvious that so long as elections remain a lottery in which a minority within a minority may take over power — which, for the period of each Parliament, is virtually unlimited — so long will there be no certainty about the future on which entrepreneurs can rely. Nor has the Government initiated the international measures which are needed if trade is to be revived.

Looking outside Britain, the world is more prosperous than it has ever been before, but the drop from rich to poor is very steep and, contrasted with the possibilities of prosperity if the advances of science were properly used, its performance is poor. Further, while expectations of greater material wealth have been aroused everywhere, the religious, moral and political climate has deteriorated. There may have been fewer major wars in the last thirty-five years than in most periods of the world's history, but those carried on by the communists in South-East Asia have been particularly pointless and frightful. If war does break out, the potential destruction is beyond contemplation. Yet the communist countries and their sympathizers in the West advocate violence as a method of government.

The world economy is in recession. The figures for the unemployed, the decrease or cessation of growth in many countries and the slowing of world trade all show that. But the recession differs from many previous recessions in several ways. In Britain we have 'stagflation'. We have constant demands for more of everything, including wages, though the extra wealth which alone can give 'more' is not being produced. Although six out of seven families are better off than they were four years ago, the morale of the nation is low. The old economic assumptions no longer hold true. For instance, a rise in monetary price does not necessarily stimulate greater production and less consumption: restrictive practices may prohibit the former, and higher pay or welfare benefits may frustrate the latter. The same is probably true throughout most of the Western world. The supposed science of macro-economics seems to me to be in the position of pre-Einstein physics. It is still true that the shortest distance between two points is a straight line, just as the theories of the free market are still true, but space now appears to be curved, so that you cannot follow the straight line, and the free market is distorted by all kinds of political pressures. The recession is not as damaging to health, food, clothing and so on in the Western world as it would have been fifty years ago. Desperate poverty exists in a few places (in southern Italy, for example) but on the whole in the industrial 'WASP' countries of the world it has been largely eliminated. Sociologists may claim that large numbers are below the 'poverty line'. But this is because in the West the 'poverty line' has been moved upwards. Meanwhile we have to compete with countries like South Korea, where the old laws of economics still apply.

What is more disturbing in the Western world and its offshoots is dissatisfaction, allied to irrationality. People who are not hungry and do not lack gadgets are not necessarily contented. Nor has prolonged education taught judgement or indeed how to enjoy life. It is impossible and unnecessary to calculate whether the taking of drugs (including alcohol and smoking) has increased per person since the eighteenth century. It certainly remains high throughout the world, and prosperity does not diminish it. As for irrationality, the admiration evinced for communism, which has proved to be the most appalling of political systems so far invented by man, is enough to demonstrate this. But if it is the most extreme example of the modern lunacy, it is by no means the only one. Even outside communist countries belief in the limitless beneficence of the state persists, in spite of the lessons of all history. We have too the widespread conviction that more money means more wealth. But the comparatively new and potent delusion is that happiness can be achieved by the realization of ambitions stimulated by advertising and the pursuit of prestige.

Of course, a small proportion of the human race has always been very ambitious. But the chasing after ill-defined (if defined at all) earthly goods, promotion, titles, medals, motor cars, on the scale on which it is practised today, is something new. The Greek ideals of restraint, of economy, of serious application to the cultivation of the mind and the Christian teaching of poverty, charity in all its senses, of self-sacrifice, indeed of the Ten Commandments, have given way in the West and in its cultural colonies overseas to the ideals of the barbarians. The individual is sacrificed to the rulers. Ostentation, unending demands, the glorification of material success have ousted to a great extent the older philosophies. The Greek and Christian ideals were never realized, but it is only comparatively recently that they have been rejected even as ideals and that whole nations have come to ape the barbarians. The high priests of barbarism were Stalin and Hitler. Stalin's ideals are still pursued in the Soviet Union and by communists all over the world. But it is not only at its extremes in the USSR and in communist South-East Asia that the ideals and methods of barbarism can be seen. The constant clamour for change, for inflation of every human activity, the uncertainty and debasement of values, the growing strength of bureaucracy as against individuality — these can be seen all over the world. It is these new attitudes, not poverty, that are now the chief menace in the West.

In the 'under-developed' world (as it is called), where poverty exists on a large scale, these attitudes are to a large extent responsible for poverty and for the desolation that goes with it. We have exported our bureaucrats' worship of the state. We have taught the rulers in Africa, Asia and South America to spend their meagre resources on arms, prestige airlines and other nationalized and grandiose schemes for the supposed glorification of those in power. We have infected them with the St Vitus dance from which we suffer. Not because familiar tools and values have ceased to be useful, not because of public demand but because of the lust for prestige change is always in process — buildings are demolished, land is covered in concrete, new fads and gadgets must be installed. It is a shameful waste in the rich countries but far worse in the poor. We have taught them and ourselves that their plight is our fault despite the billions of pounds handed over to their governments. We have not taught them to study Japan and other countries which have pulled themselves up to prosperity. It would be a difficult lesson to teach. The lust for power is more virulent than the lust for money. It can be contained only within a community in which law and restraint are recognized. That is not the kind of community which often exists in Africa, Asia or South America. Dictators are no more addicted to tolerance than are alcoholics to water.

As for war, we live under the threat of Russian aggression and the violent doctrine of communism. Wars may and do erupt for other reasons (the Iraqi—Iranian war, the invasion of Lebanon by Israel), but any wars in Europe or a world war would be due to the imperialist dictatorship of Russia. So far deterrence has helped to keep the peace in Europe for thirty-seven years. It remains the policy of the Alliance, and I believe that is right. How it should be maintained is discussed later. Here it is relevant to point out that deterrence requires a considerable allocation of resources and the will to maintain large conventional forces.

What has been the response of the Liberal Party to the history of Britain, her Governments and world developments since the war? Some years ago I wrote two books, *The Liberal Future* and *The Liberal Challenge*. More recently I have written *The Common Welfare*. They set out my views. Books by active Liberal politicians about Liberalism have been comparatively rare of recent years, but there has been a large output of liberal writing. To my mind the party has not paid sufficient attention to the ideas, not all new but many of them interesting in a new context, which have been promulgated by such writers as F.A. Hayek, Ralph Harris, Arthur Seldon and others associated with the Institute of Economic Affairs, Norman Macrae and contributors to the *Economist*, Robert Oakeshott and others interested in the co-operative movement, the new publicists in America, Alan Peacock, Sam Brittan and the large number of liberal economists. The leadership of the party has not over the last twelve or fifteen years shown much interest in new radical political or economic thought. It has been concerned with some important social issues, such as abortion, apartheid and race relations. Otherwise the party has concentrated on current issues as they have arisen, on an attempt to increase representation in Parliament and on local authorities. For the latter purpose in particular it has developed what it describes as 'community politics'. I am certainly sympathetic to this move. I remember saying many years ago that any local Liberal who got a bus stop moved did more good for the cause than fifty speeches. *The Common Welfare* was partly an attempt to develop a theory of community action designed as an alternative to state socialism and as a means of raising the standards of the poor communities. But that theme has not been taken up. When Liberals speak of community action they usually mean raising grievances and pressing for action by an organization, either the state or the local authority, to be financed by national taxation. It has not stressed enough the positive role of local people, nor the desirability of forgoing state assistance on some occasions. I have always believed that politics are partly about protest. The Members of the House of Commons were traditionally elected not to govern but to prevent too much government, to stand in opposition to government, criticizing and thwarting it. So I am sympathetic, up to a point, with modern protest politics. But a great deal of modern protest, the constant complaint in the local sheets usually called *Focus* which Liberals have been producing, is that government is not doing enough. This campaign is exactly the opposite of the original protest made by the Members sent up from the shires and cities of England: it is usually a plea for more government and more expenditure.

However, in local government the Liberal Party has been very successful in recent years. From a few scattered councillors, it has grown to a position where, over large areas of Britain, it is not far behind the other parties. From being confined to the smaller towns and rural areas, it now is the second largest party, and the governing one, in Liverpool and is represented on the councils of most of the big cities. This is a welcome development and should be exploited. The party's smaller success in national elections is also welcome. Its vote is notoriously unreflected by the number of seats won. The gross distortion caused by our electoral system makes it difficult to assess its potential strength, but this appears to lie in the work of local associations and in the appeal of Jeremy

Thorpe and particularly of David Steel at General Elections rather than in the conversion of large numbers to the principles of Liberalism. Having passed through a period when the party accused the Tory and Labour parties of being identical twins, it has lately proclaimed that they are pulling apart in a way which does not represent the true needs or wishes of the nation. Liberal leaders have denounced adversarial politics, the chopping and changing which they claim to perceive when a new party takes office, the disruption of the nation and the aggravation of the antipathy between the two sides of industry. This being a theme congenial to the Social Democrat leadership, it has to be examined very seriously before any assessment is made of what the Alliance can or is likely to do.

Is the claim true? To some extent it is. But the polarization of which Liberals complain is partly the result of the failure of the moderate left to develop a liberal philosophy in political terms. As the Labour Party has had no new thought beyond bureaucratic state socialism, and is indeed prevented from having any such thought by its dependence on the trade unions, the Marxists have had the political field to themselves. They have certainly injected a note of extremism into politics — for instance, by their rejection of the presuppositions of democracy and, indeed, of democracy itself. It is also true that the failure of the 1945—60 consensus to deal with inflation, unemployment and the weight of the welfare state has made the vested interests which have grown around the consensus somewhat desperate. The Conservative Government of the last four years has for its part appeared to cling to a position which has been widely denounced as doctrinaire and for which a great part of the nation is unprepared.

But I cannot say that I find the present Government to be composed òf ferocious right-wing radicals. Their predecessors were forced to curtail the money supply. In the aftermath of the locust years and in the face of a world slump I doubt if any Government could have prevented a high level of unemployment, even temporarily, except at the cost of ruinous inflation. Certainly, some of the Government's measures have been ill-judged, but the most serious criticism that the Tories have to face is that they have failed to tackle the structure of the country. They have done too little, not too much, to change the nationalized industries. (Here I disagree with those Liberals who would leave the mix of the mixed economy as it is now.) Nor have the Tories changed the machinery of government, the voting system, the structure of industry or the welfare state. They have not in fact, whatever they promised, slashed the size of government. These matters will be dealt with in more detail below. I mention them here to cast doubt on the Liberal, and indeed the Alliance, diagnosis of our troubles in this respect.

Looking back over the time that I have spent in the House of Commons, I can detect three phases in the history of the Liberal Party. After the war, bereft of the old leaders and reduced to a handful of Members, we were groping for a position in British politics. I characterized the party as a non-socialist radical party anchored to the belief that it was the individual in the community who is the foundation of politics. We attracted enterprising business advisers and many able academics in all sorts of disciplines — economics, foreign affairs, defence and politics themselves. Then came the era of organization. Now, with the rise of the Alliance, the radical thought of the late 1950s and 1960s should be revived and integrated with the organization which has been built up. To my mind, the failure of the Labour Party has been partly a failure to develop new ideas or to recast old ideas in the new setting in which we live. I do not believe that such a process can be achieved by committees. The leadership of a party has many roles. One is to keep in touch, possibly through intermediaries, with what is going on in areas where innovation is taking place. It is in these areas that the seeds of further advances are sown. Innovations do not win votes at the time of innovation, but they attract lively minds and can inspire the next generation of active politicians.

I have outlined my view of the history of British politics since the war and touched on the international setting. From this it will be seen that in my view much more is needed than a return to some middle-of-the-road policy embracing the social services, financial and fiscal methods, the mixed economy and the role of the state as they exist today. It may be that practical questions of organization which have absorbed most of the energy of the

Liberal Party have been necessary. But the absence of new political thought among the leaders of the party and their failure, as I judge it, to engage the new thought outside the party have very nearly, if not quite, handed over the running on the radical side of politics to the younger Tories. Liberal policy formation has been farmed out to various panels or committees. My experience is that the most creative thinkers either will not or cannot always give much time to such committees. The leadership, having decided what it wants, has to go out and pick the brains of individuals who are most likely to make a contribution. Nor, democratic though it may be, is the Assembly or the Council meeting a suitable instrument of policy formulation.

The leadership of the Alliance must now tap the various sources of new ideas that are compatible with its aims, which are, first, to inject more populism into the existing Establishment and, secondly, to decentralize from Whitehall and Westminster — and I mean decentralize structurally as well as geographically. These points seem compatible with its published proposals. Its task is to create what might be called a form of socialism without the state. This will entail convincing the electorate that it — or the bulk of it — will gain from the pursuit of policies of benefit to us all. The classical method of achieving this is to harness self-interest through the market. I see no better way, given five conditions.

The first is parity of esteem. Everyone, whether he or she is successful in the market or not, is primarily a human being and has a life to live. The second is that everyone should have some muscle power. That is to say, not only should there be the celebrated 'net' to hold up the poor and unlucky but also every child should have an opportunity to choose and to take part in the running of the country's affairs, not only by voting a couple of times in five years. (For this reason I greatly regret that the ownership of North Sea oil was not split up among us all. Perhaps we could have a national endowment?) Producers' co-operation and all forms of partnership should be encouraged. Third, a clear distinction should be made between business which can and should be subject to the market and those services which should not. The latter should be run with quite different motives. They should be directly under democratic control. Fourth, there should be small but strong authorities — state and local — controlling a sector comprising not more than 20 per cent of the economy. Fifth, children should be taught the need for some common bonds of belief quite separate from the bonds of institutional member-ship. The paradox of the plural society, or of socialism without the state but with the market, is that it can exist only if there is some morality that is generally accepted, though no doubt often ignored, some willingness to sacrifice personal gain to a common good, some leadership to guide behaviour and some mutual trust. Unless you have certain bonds, some natural cohesion, you are thrown back on force of one kind or another. The individual surrenders to the group, union, organization; these in turn battle for all they can get. Anarchy results until resolved by dictatorship.

The current views of the Alliance leadership are already on record. Dr David Owen, Mr William Rodgers and Mrs Shirley Williams have written books. Mr Roy Jenkins has deployed his policies at two by-elections and Mr Steel his in many speeches. Already several reports have issued from both the Liberal Party and the SDP, and there is a growing mass of Liberal resolutions. The salient features of Alliance policies would seem to be a resurg-ence of Keynesian economics coupled with an incomes policy, electoral reform, some measure of inflation and increased capital spending, regional councils in England, Scottish and Welsh devolu-tion within the UK and a firm commitment to the EEC, NATO and the nuclear deterrent. So far the Alliance leaders have made no official proposals for reforming the nationalized industries or the public sector generally. It seems that they will not denationalize any part of the state industries. David Owen in his book speaks well of producer co-operatives, but up to now the Alliance policy state-ments say nothing of introducing such co-operatives into the state sector. Mr Rodgers writes persuasively about the trade unions. In *The Politics of Change* he says:

> Strong trades unionism must never betray its traditional goals, prosperity, fraternity, security, fairness and justice. That requirement demands that unions assess their actions by broader criteria than the short-term interests of particular sections of their membership. (p. 103)

If the trade unions are to follow Mr Rodgers's advice, they must look favourably on new forms of industrial organization. In the long run the Alliance must produce new thought about the size and management of the public sector and the structure of politics.

Much as I agree with some of the Alliance Green Papers, I hope that this book will make a contribution to the debate about Alliance policies from a different angle. I hesitate to call it a specifically Liberal angle because that might imply that I judge the SDP to be illiberal, which I certainly do not, or that I can speak for the Liberal Party, which I cannot. But I have had a different experience of politics from that of the Gang of Four and their followers and inevitably see some things from a different point of view.

It is no criticism of the current policies of the Alliance to say that they could be accepted by Tory 'wets'. The Alliance has welcomed ex-Tories into its ranks. I myself, in proposing a realignment of our politics many years ago, suggested a party including the left of the Tory Party as well as Liberal and moderate Labour members.

But things have moved on. If my analysis of our recent history and present situation is right, we have to deal with a different Britain from that in which I first advocated realignment. Since the 1960s we have seen state socialism in practice and in its inability to generate new thought. We have seen the rise of extreme socialism as the philosophy of active Labour supporters. We have seen the growth of bureaucracy and the malfunctioning of the mixed economy. We know that the social services, as at present organized, are not solving social problems or promoting equality. They have become infinitely complicated and expensive. Though I believe that the Alliance must appeal to moderate voters, therefore, I do not believe that it can rely indefinitely on policies which seek only to ameliorate and modify or represent a partial return to the nostrums which have proved ineffective. I hope that the Liberal element in the Alliance will inject new and radical thought about changes in the general mould of our society.

Britain now is similar in many respects to nineteenth-century Spain or early twentieth-century Austria, countries living in the twilight of empire, not without eruptions of genius but politically torpid under a complacent bureaucracy. She is, by her geography and her dependence on international trade, unsuited to a regime of benign incompetence. But if the Alliance is to rouse her, the task will be a difficult one, calling for some galvanic stimulation.

Reviewing the System
of Government

2

Local Government

Before embarking on any change it is wise to ask: what is wrong? What is the mischief that we are trying to cure? What is wrong with our system of government?

I am predisposed to look at our system by starting at the local level and working upwards.

At the local level what is at fault is the growth of bureaucratic attitudes, the failure to define the scope of local government, the confusion between local and central government and the lack of a reasonable system of local government finance. I would like to be able to leave to neighbourhoods all the powers that they can discharge, reserving to the upper tiers of government only matters which must clearly be handled on a wider basis. In my book *The Common Welfare* my thesis was that the country should rest on three pillars: a free market, the community and workers' participation in, or ownership of, industry, all kept in balance by a strong central government. This government, I argued, should be charged not only with foreign affairs, defence, overall planning and economic management, but also with ensuring that the poor do not go to the wall and that no subordinate authority oversteps its powers. The central administration, though strong, should have a narrower remit than it has today. In fact, I am in favour of small, strong government in place of the present dropsical animal which envelops more than it assists.

But since writing *The Common Welfare* I have had to think again. The conduct of some local authorities makes me chary about giving them any more power. One argument for greater local autonomy was the persistent gap between incomes, welfare

and education in the industrial areas of, for example, the north of
Scotland, Wales, Northern Ireland and those in certain areas of
south-eastern England and neighbourhoods elsewhere that are
inhabited largely by retired families and office workers. I detect
that the policy of uniformity, which imposes the same standards
and the same methods of education and public administration
all over Britain, has failed. (There are, of course, differences in the
methods adopted in Scotland and, to a small extent, elsewhere.)
Certainly, the child in Unst, Shetland, has a right to similar services, similar health care and education, say, as the child in London
or Brighton, but I do not believe that rigid uniformity is practicable. However hard we may try to make all of Britain conform
to a pattern, we cannot do it. And if we could do it, it would
be a pattern to suit London, not Unst, so we might as well transport the Unstmen south. I am convinced that the troubles of
Scotland, of the Clyde, of Swansea or the Hebrides spring from
the attempt to dictate from the centre, even though the central
administration has tried to confer benefits on the poorer areas. It
seems to me, therefore, that the principle should be not imposition
of the same pattern throughout Britain but assistance to every
community to go its own way and develop its own way of life.

But there are grounds for caution. First, some local authorities
have caught bureaucratic blight and suffer from delusions of
grandeur in a big way. They pursue ends which suit themselves
but not necessarily their constituents. They tend not to try to
develop a way of life of their own. They demand resources from
central government so that their staffs, buildings and general
expenditure keep abreast or ahead of those of other councils.
They grasp at current fashions. They imitate each other. They are
not keen to follow a judgement of what their areas can achieve
by actions attuned to achieve it. By dabbling in all kinds of
activity, they divert energy and money from the needs and possibilities of their area. They are apt to become both incompetent
and extravagant. Second, there is the polarization of political
loyalties in some parts of Britain and the domination of some
councils by one party. The Tory minority in some London boroughs
and the Labour minority in Bournemouth have little more hope of
power-sharing than had the Northern Irish Roman Catholics. In

some areas there is no community in the sense of common loyalties and some consensus on how the neighbourhood should be governed. Third, local authority spending now imposes a heavy burden upon the national budget.

Nevertheless, I cling to my belief in local autonomy. Sterner limits must be set on what local authorities can and cannot do. (By 'do' I mean do themselves or get done for them.) This would not be necessary if local electors took a more active interest in their localities. Interest might be stimulated and a bigger turn-out at local elections prompted if local authorities had to raise their finance by methods which impinged more directly on all their electorates. But even if a better method of local government finance could be found — a topic to be discussed below — I think that we must define the powers of local authorities more closely in the light of recent experience.

Local authorities should be responsible for the provision of police, fire and refuse collection services. These are services which largely serve the common good. Though refuse collection might well be farmed out to contractors or co-operatives, yet to my mind some public authority should have the duty of overseeing it. It would also be convenient perhaps to place under the aegis of local authorities other services which provide broadly common benefits — matters, for instance, of hygiene and preventative medicine. There is then an almost indefinitely extensible range of activities which offer certain common benefits. Of these education is one important example. If different parts of Great Britain are to be encouraged to develop their own personalities, so to speak, education will be important to them. Children must be taught both an appreciation of the peculiar possibilities and opportunities of their home and skills appropriate to life there. On the other hand, one of the easiest ways to relieve local authorities of some expenditure would be to pay teachers' salaries from the Exchequer. An educational system which opens up adequate chances in tertiary education must have some uniformity. Not every local authority could run its own university. It seems to me that responsibility for primary and secondary education, subject to a central inspectorate in each of England, Scotland, Wales and Northern Ireland, should remain with the local authorities.

Transport and development present difficulties. I have argued in *The Common Welfare* and in speeches that both in some ways impinge on the social services. Not only in rural areas and islands but also in towns transport is essential to a decent life. As individuals become richer and we move over to a minimum income, they should be able to pay out of their own pockets for an adequate transport system. But until that desirable state of affairs is reached, what should we do? Local councillors are not elected for their ability to run enterprises — nor are officials likely to be adept at the efficient provision of transport. If left in their hands, it is all too likely to become an ever more highly subsidized vested interest. For the moment, however, I think that local authorities must retain power to subsidize transport, though some limit should be imposed on the amount of money that they can spend in this way.

As for development, every local authority today is bent on promoting its area as a site for industry or a heaven for tourists. Local councils employ not only development officers of various kinds but also agricultural and other advisers. I do not doubt that a thriving means of livelihood in its midst is a boon to any neighbourhood, but I now see the foolishness with which authorities embark on ventures, knowing that it is the ratepayers or the Treasury that will suffer if they fail. I note the rash belief they have in their own or their officials' capacity to take on more and more jobs in fields for which they are untrained. I fear that one of the mistakes of the nationalization and planning measures of 1945 will be repeated at the local level. Most members of the 1945 Parliament must have known from personal experience that any business run by a public authority which belongs to no one, in which the management is not constrained by fear of losing money on a market, in which bills will always eventually be met by the taxpayer, is strongly tempted to be inefficient. Yet they devised no safeguards. The nationalized industries, unlike the Army, were not to be public services under discipline. They were to be monopoly businesses without any of the spurs and checks which keep business efficient. They were never to be allowed to go bankrupt. Nor did the Labour Party of 1945 look around it and ask if Parliament was capable of supervising such businesses. If it was not capable, to whom were they to be responsible?

Are local authorities any better equipped to manage business than was the 1945 Parliament? The answer must be no. But yet if a community is falling into poverty and despair for lack of employment, surely it should be allowed to seek and support any that it can get? And if a community feels that it has potential in some direction, why should it not be allowed to exploit it? The danger is that each community vies with its neighbour in attempting to attract business, with the possibility of beggaring us all. Nevertheless, I think that this is an argument for caution, not despair.

I incline to think that development is something which a community should be able to pursue, but not necessarily through its local council. Some large authorities should retain their development powers; others should rely on regional bodies such as the Highlands and Islands Development Board. As I suggest in another chapter, local boards should be set up that are equipped not only to provide local finance for local enterprise but also to supervise and assist local business. When this comes about, the local community will have some influence over the development of its area through such boards. Possibly these bodies should have directly elected members on their boards.

In chapter 6, on social services, I explain that I would hope to see the social services declining as prosperity spreads. I would also hope to see them taken over by co-operatives, of which the recipients of services were members. This would remove them from the direct management of local authorities. I do not see the need for an absolutely uniform system of services. In some areas charities or co-operative groups may be the right way to run old folk's homes and canteens, home-helps and so on; in others the local inhabitants may prefer to act through their authorities. In any event, I am in favour of personal social services being handled locally not centrally — indeed, I favour giving local authorities the power to decide, within limits, the types of service to be provided.

As for housing, as soon as it was practicable I would hand this over to local housing co-operatives in so far as it cannot be provided by owner-occupation. The poor, until we raise lower incomes, can be helped by subsidies. I am in favour of helping the tenant, not the house. I can see no reason why rich tenants should be assisted through the holding down of council house rents. In fact, while I have not lost my enthusiasm for community self-determination, the experience of the last three years has inclined me to think that it should not be sought entirely through the delegation of unlimited powers to local authorities.

The most vexatious matter entrusted to local authorities is planning. I do not doubt that some control must be exercised over buildings and the use of land; nor do I doubt that this must be done locally. But the results of the planning laws of the central government can be seen all over the country. Bad planning has laid waste the cities, urbanized villages and led to the follies of structure plans and zoning. The planning laws should be reduced in scope, and more discretion should be left to local authorities. The same planning laws cannot make sense all over the country.

To end this brief discussion about what local authorities can and cannot do, one further point needs to be made. Local authorities should be debarred from activities that extend beyond the boundaries of the community — dabbling in the affairs of Northern Ireland, for instance.

I now come to the all-important matter of local government finance. If communities are to be free to make the best of themselves, they must be prepared to pay the bulk of the cost (except in a few special and probably temporary cases). Apart from the justice of this proposition, I do not believe that communities that rely indefinitely on subsidies to meet the great part of their expenditure will ever make the best of themselves. Having to find the money would also wonderfully concentrate the minds of local councillors upon priorities.

What do we require of a system of local finance, bearing in mind what I hold should be the aim of local authorities? In some discussions about local taxation it has been suggested that it should be as painless as possible. I dissent. I believe that the exemption, or near exemption, of so many people from the burden of the rates is a cause of waste in local government. The outcry of ratepayers can be salutary. I believe that any form of local taxation should be felt, and clearly felt, by nearly all the population in the area — though in varying degrees. I am not wholly averse to a poll-tax for this reason, if it were to be kept low. I am modestly in favour of some form of indirect tax, in spite of the opposition it arouses. It seems to me that it might be no bad thing if people found that by taking the bus for a mile or two they could buy cheaper beer or cigarettes in a neighbouring authority. In the USA sales tax varies from place to place, though of course the units are bigger. I know the objections to local indirect taxation, but then all taxes have their drawbacks. Indirect taxes have the advantage of being clearly seen. If they are levied on such things as beer, tobacco or sweets, they can be evaded by the poor or strong-minded. If they are resented, the electors have the choice of electing councillors who will spend less money.

However, I am impressed by the comparative simplicity of the flat percentage tax, as levied on the Isle of Man. Every citizen or married couple in business on the Isle of Man is issued with a single-page document on which to enter earnings, various deductions (for example, for children) and expenses incurred in earning the income. There are also certain reliefs for age, low income and so on. After all these deductions have been subtracted from income, the residue is taxed at a rate fixed annually. This system was only introduced a few years ago, and some further study should be made of its effects, but it would seem to have many advantages as a method of raising local taxation.

The alternative is some form of local income tax, which seems a possibility subject to three conditions: it must reach fairly far down the income range; it must be clearly seen to be related to local expenditure; and some ceiling must be imposed on the total amount of tax, national and local, which is levied. I confess that I suspect that these three criteria would be difficult to meet. I also suspect that any local income tax would simply be added to national income taxation; few people would be clear about the difference between them; and the tax would eventually be thought as unfair as the rates.

The rating system is perhaps not quite as bad as it is made out to be. For instance, it is alleged that companies pay large rates but have no representation on local authorities — but they pay corporation and other taxes, yet have no representation in Parliament either. What does seem to me questionable is that businesses should be allowed to offset rates against taxation. This militates against the new or struggling business, and it is a boon denied to individual ratepayers. At present the rates are comparatively easy to collect and the ratepayer is only too well aware of how he stands. Nevertheless, the system is grossly unfair, and on balance I would hope that the Alliance would abandon it in favour of either a flat percentage tax or a local income tax if local indirect taxes would seem too much of an affront to our susceptibilities.

3

Central Government and Parliamentary Reform

In my experience the grievance most frequently brought before MPs is that the Government is not doing or spending enough. The plea for more government action and expenditure is made by individuals in some cases but most constantly by the innumerable pressure groups whose activity has grown so enormously since the Second World War. They include charities, trade organizations, the professions, the trade unions, local authorities, public boards, universities, quangos, associations and institutions of every kind. They all have staffs of one kind or another. A prime occupation of each staff is to press for 'more' — more money, more legislation, more public regulation and expenditure, more perks, more power. Even the Consumers' Association often asks for more regulations to protect consumers. I am not for the moment arguing whether or not this pressure for more government action is justified. All I am saying is that an immense number of organizations now exist to promote it and, by their very nature, will never be satisfied that enough has been done. To admit this would be to put themselves out of a job. To counter the pressure on the Government to do more there is a much less articulate cry that it is doing too much; a small committee in the House of Lords inspired by Lord Harris of High Cross, some individual MPs, some councillors and perhaps the Freedom Association are about the only campaigners against more legislation. Every Government sooner or later has to draw in its horns, not because the bureaucracies of the country demand this but because the pressures of life compel it to do so.

A major fault of Britain is that her capacity for spending has outrun her capacity for production. That her citizens, at least as they are represented by the organizations into which they are marshalled, constantly demand more expenditure and more regulation is due largely to four causes. First, there is the separation between taxation and public expenditure, so that the organization which, say, demands better housing for single immigrants does not have to find the money. Second, there is the fear of being left behind: if I or my organization do not demand more, someone else will get to the trough ahead of us. Third, there are the demands of the various bureaucracies, often shielded by cheap mortgages, perks, indexed salaries and pensions from the inflation to which their rapacity leads. And, last, there is the indoctrination of children and adults by education, advertising and the bureaux that they are entitled to 'more'. A country whose demands constantly outrun its ability to meet them cannot be healthy. The cure, however, must lie in changed attitudes and a reformed structure of government. Attempts to prune the existing jungle of expenditure are futile. As Alan Peacock and Jack Wiseman point out in their book *The Growth of Public Expenditure in the United Kingdom* — a cautionary tale that all should read — 'Citizens can have ideas about desirable public expenditure which are quite different from, and incompatible with, their ideas about responsible burdens of taxation.'*

We might indeed say, therefore, that a major fault of our political system is that there is no balance between what organizations of all kinds want and the capacity of the country to choose which demands should be satisfied with a view to the common good.

It used to be the job of Parliament, particularly of the House of Commons, to curb the powers and expenditures of Governments. MPs were sent up to Westminster to keep an eye on the ambitions of the executive. They were not there to vote money for the executive to spend until the grievances of their constituents had been met. To expect MPs to press for more government action and expenditure is to turn their traditional task upside down. MPs are well aware that they make a poor job of containing govern-

---

* Princeton: Princeton University Press for the National Bureau of Economic Research, 1966, p. xxiv.

ment expenditure. They do not feel that the House of Commons as such is able to examine the way in which our enormous budget is spent. They foster a contradiction of their own here. They have set up various committees to enable government expenditure to be more closely examined, but at the same time, at the request of lobbyists, they press constantly for more of it. What they mean by the control of government expenditure is largely the control of administrative costs, the elimination of waste, scrutiny to ensure that money voted for a particular purpose is used for that purpose. That seems laudable as far as it goes, but is not such scrutiny like a drug which lulls but does not cure? I sometimes wonder whether accountability, like accountants, is not one of the burdens upon the back of Britain — or a distraction from a proper examination of what is wrong. Accountability to a market, yes. Accountability to a senior officer who may impose punishments, yes too. But accountability in the form of reports which can be tailored to examiners who are probably ignorant, much more doubtful. It may in the end waste time and discourage initiative. It does not redress the serious mischief which has dogged Britain since the war, the growth of bureaucratic attitudes resulting in the constant tendency for Governments to spend more than the country earns.

At the level of central government the constant tendency for expenditure to overrun production is, as I have said, one of the principal sources of trouble. And a prime cause of this tendency is the pressure of interest groups of all kinds. In recent years every Government has faced the dilemma of either accepting the demands of some powerful group, with consequent inflation, or enduring a damaging strike.

How do we meet this dilemma? One way is to accept it — to accept that corporatism is here to stay, that it should be brought further out into the light of day and subjected to examination by the press and Parliament. It might be that by forcing them to debate their demands in public we would check the voracity of bureaucracies. We might breed antibodies in the body politic.

It is worth noting here that could we arrange for institutions to be dedicated to higher output and efficiency, there would be much to be said for their representation in Parliament. It could well be argued that our trouble is not excessive demand but inadequate supply. Unfortunately, such institutions hardly exist. At the political level the pressure is all for expenditure, not improved productivity.

As with Keynesian and monetarist theories, the issue of corporatism must be recognized and defined. The Alliance must not pretend that it does not exist. After both parties have looked the matter in the face, it may be possible for them to handle it without wholly accepting or rejecting the rights of corporate institutions.

The issue has various facets. Do we think of society as made up of individuals or of institutions of which those individuals are members? Universities, political parties, trade unions, organizations of merchants, lawyers and many other professions have played an important and often valuable part in our history. The free world must admire the Polish trade unions. I do not accept that without the growth of trade unions in the nineteenth century the workers would have won better wages and conditions. The universities have been admirable centres of teaching and research. In fact, it is difficult to envisage a satisfactory society without institutions, but that does not mean that the particular form in which they now exist is the best one. When at their most laudable, institutions have increased the potential of their members, who have been able both to enhance their own opportunities and to contribute to the general welfare through those institutions. My criticism is not that all institutions are bad — far from it — but that ours are in need of reform. Institutions should be the servants, not the masters, of individuals. They should not absorb individuals so that the latter are reduced to playing roles and are inhibited from being all-round men and women.

Another facet of the issue is the relationship between the institution and the general good. Is it the business of the institution simply to press the interests of its members, leaving it to other institutions or the state to fix limits for its success? This question leads to a consideration of whether the officials of institutions are bound by morality. Are they moral entities, as individuals are? Or is it the duty of their officials simply to fight their corner? Further, the officials of institutions today are inclined to fight for their own interests as officials rather than for those of their members. Very few institutions are prepared to accept a curtailment of their officials' power, let alone to liquidate themselves even though this might be in the interests of their members.

To me it is a cardinal error of Labour Party leaders and some Conservatives to assert that the present form of our institutions is almost perfect. While, therefore, I accept that we must recognize institutions as an essential part of our constitution, I do not go on to recommend a further increase in their powers. They should be subject to the general law of the land. Their voices should be heard, but they must acquiesce to the general authority of a Parliament elected by individuals as individuals.

The rejection of corporatism may seem a reactionary conclusion. It can be argued that such rejection is an attempt to return to a type of democracy which is no longer feasible, that it would be more realistic to have, say, the trade unions directly and openly represented in Parliament, since many Members of Parliament sit there because of trade union support. It can be said – and I have said it – that many constituencies do not coincide with communities which share common interests. We might just as well vote according to the initial letters of our names. If this position is thought too extreme, at least the second chamber should be a corporate chamber. There is a long tradition of the representation of different estates of the realm. So, some say, let us have a second chamber to which the Confederation of British Industry (CBI), the trade unions, the universities and others elect members.

This line of reasoning is compelling only for conservatives, who assume that the present organizations and outlook of the country must continue. But I must say again that the Alliance must break other moulds besides the political one. Its view of the country must embrace all its activities. Would we need special trade union or employer representation in Parliament if, by means of new structures in industry, we could escape from the conflict between owners, managers and workers in industry? If the functions of the state were reduced, would every institution need to be in a position to fight against the state's encroachment on its independence? If every individual were guaranteed a minimum income and if we achieved a more egalitarian society, would we need representatives in government fighting exclusively for certain categories of the less fortunate?

The modern corporate institution has become almost a pressure group. Less and less does it enforce standards. The pressure which it applies is directed to extracting more from taxation through the Government. It is increasingly dependent. Though often critical of the Government, it sees its job as being to use and influence the Government. Many of those who rightly stress the important part that organizations have played in our history ignore the change that has occurred in their nature.

I therefore reject corporatism. I do so for three reasons. First, I dislike the Fascist/communist doctrine that individuals do not matter. Secondly, I believe that it is sufficient to assert the general interest. I do not believe that it is sufficient to find some compromise between sectional interests. Thirdly, I find it impossible to judge which organizations should be directly represented in Parliament. This is partly because there are so many organizations and partly because those which were represented would tend to resist all change. Suppose, for instance, it was decided that the Trades Union Congress (TUC) and the General Council of the English Bar were to be represented; this would block the way to reform of industrial relations or the law. Experience shows that the representatives would never be replaced, so that we should have one more obstacle to add to the many which already obstruct fluidity in our system. Experience also shows that if organizations such as the CBI and the TUC were represented in a second chamber, it is unlikely that their ablest members would play much part in the deliberations of that chamber. There are plenty of trade-union-sponsored MPs in the House of Commons but no leading members of the TUC.

Among the organizations which exert the heaviest pressure for expenditure are the big-spending agencies and subordinate authorities that are themselves the creation of Governments. The local authorities, the health service, the armed services, the water boards and indeed many of the nationalized industries do not pay their own way. Should they, then, have a say, through Parliament, in how money raised by taxation is spent? I think not. It is not suggested, so far as I know, that they should be directly represented in Parliament. But their activities are potent examples of corporatism.

I conclude that while institutions which maintain skills or values of their own and are not mere parliamentary pressure groups, especially those independent of government, are much to be desired, not even they — and still less most modern corporations — require positions of greater influence in our affairs, though by all means let them be consulted.

If the House of Commons is now not a very enthusiastic champion of the general interest, neither is its counterpart, the Government. The Ministries themselves are interests fighting for the segments of government that they represent and for their own employees. The Prime Minister and the Treasury are the main defenders of the general interest. This may well be taken as a reason for strengthening the central core of government. If my analysis is right, then it could be argued that we do not need further devolution or any increase in the power of the House of Commons. But for other reasons we do need to shore up populist democracy and to establish more potent control over the executive.

There are, I believe, certain measures which could be taken to promote the general interest. One is to reform and strengthen the second chamber in such a way that it is not subject to the pressures of diverse interests. A second is to make it illegal for any individual or organization to pay an MP, whether by way of salary, contribution to his party, retaining fees or the provision of assistance (for example, secretarial help). Now that MPs are paid a salary on which they can live and have generous grants for secretarial assistance, travelling and so on, it is certainly much less necessary that they should supplement what the state pays to and for them. However, an objection to this is that it would discriminate unfairly in favour of those who make money outside the House of Commons as barristers, directors, broadcasters, etc. As I am in favour of MPs having outside interests if so inclined, I find this last a cogent argument. However, as the SDP, in breaking away from the Labour Party, has also broken away from trade union sponsorship, I believe that when electoral reform is considered the desirability of abolishing trade union pocket boroughs should be borne in mind.

A third, and more drastic, innovation would be to sever the Government from membership of Parliament, as is done in the USA. As Ministers would not have to seek election, this might reduce the pressures upon them. In the long run we may have to adopt some such system, although I do not see it as a practical proposal at present. Fourth, the growth of specialist committees may help to establish a House of Commons, and possibly a national, point of view. Members of these committees, working together away from the party hysteria often to be seen and heard on the floor of the chamber, develop new loyalties and a common approach. Fifth, there is the need to relate expenditure more directly to revenue. Improvements in this direction have been made but have a long way to go yet. We still behave like a family which goes on a shopping spree one week and purchases a new car, a television and clothes with a credit card and then a week later considers its bank balance.

None of these suggestions will cure the fissiparous tendencies of the bureaucracies, but I shall return to this point when I have considered other grievances about the performance of government and Parliament.

One of these is that government is too remote, too unresponsive to the wishes of the electorate. Much legislation appears to bear little relation to what people want. The demonstrations and strikes, the sporadic outbreaks of violence in the United Kingdom and the thuggery in Northern Ireland seem to support the view that many people are frustrated. It may be that they think that a show of force is more likely to be heeded than rational argument and that the parliamentary process does not meet their needs. Television and the press have exacerbated this trend. Television needs pictures of people doing things. A disturbance is more likely to make headline news than a cogent argument. It is not certain therefore that improvements in Parliament's sensitivity to public opinion will necessarily meet what is thought to be the need. I say 'what is thought to be' for much of the frustration is confined to groups who do not represent majority opinion. Parliamentary democracy, while it must lean over to pay attention to minorities, ultimately depends upon majority rule. Further, we have again to cope with the tendency of many groups to seek influence through local authorities and organizations, thereby to some extent by-passing the House of Commons.

The fault here seems to lie chiefly with the old party system, in itself a grievance. As they have been constituted, the parties tend to repress certain subjects of importance because to have them debated in Parliament would be an embarrassment. This occurs when parties are divided on an issue (for example, unilateral nuclear disarmament) or when neither the Tory nor the Labour Party wishes to come clean (for example, over some industrial disputes). And while many issues that are of importance to the public are not tackled, Parliament is dogged by legislation that is often footling and frequently actually absurd. Moreover, the party system is largely to blame for the under-representation of women in the House of Commons, since the parties have consistently failed to attract or to adopt women candidates. The SDP has already set an example by ensuring that there are equal numbers of men and women on the executive.

The Alliance represents a break with the dominance of politics by two parties, one kept in existence almost entirely by the trade unions, the other largely dependent on employers. The Alliance, being free of dependence on either the trade unions or big business, should be able to broaden the base of our politics.

A third failing which I diagnose is the difficulty that democratically elected Ministers experience in controlling their own bureaucracies and experts. Science and technology constantly advance. Judgement as to how they are to be used should be within the capacity of those trained to judge. To be able to express an informed opinion about their use it is not necessary to be a master of advanced science, but it is necessary to have been trained in judgement. It is also necessary to have all the relevant evidence laid before you in a manner which makes correct judgement possible. The judgement of Ministers and MPs may be defective, but I doubt if their Civil Service advisers are capable of serving up technical matters for them in a form which makes for rational decision-making.

Where does consideration of these failings lead us? Certainly to the view that there is too much government. The first elementary and most pressing need is to declare a moratorium on all portmanteau Bills while examining how many Acts and regulations can be repealed. I suspect that such happy hunting-grounds for officials as the fire regulations have got wholly out of hand.

Having, I hope (though I hope with no great certainty), achieved a change of attitude and curbed the propensity of the bureaux to promote legislation, the Alliance must turn to political reform. This is now urgent. It is a field entirely neglected by the Labour Party and the Conservatives. Mrs Thatcher's Government, having extended the committee system, has wholly ignored this issue. Yet it is the vital one, for most of our troubles spring from political, not economic, causes.

At the top of the agenda of political reform stands the need for electoral reform. The excessive power of organizations and the dissatisfaction of the citizen with the remoteness and often apparent irrevelance or oppressiveness of government are all to some extent due to the present electoral system.

The arguments for the first-past-the-post, single-Member constituency are that it simplifies politics and that it shows where responsibility lies. Of these the second is, to me, much the more compelling. I value the link which binds each Member to his constituents. If Members are remote now, they would perhaps be even more remote if constituencies were tripled in size and each was represented by three MPs. I do not attach much importance, if any, to the argument about stable government. Stable government is not necessarily threatened by coalitions. On the contrary, the stability and political success of West Germany is partly due to the balance that the Free Democrats have lent to successive coalitions. What must damage democratic politics is the lottery run under the present system. That no Government represents a majority of the nation, that a party with the most votes can emerge without a majority in the Commons and that a minority of extremists within a minority may end up in power must be wrong and could be very dangerous. The need for change is made more urgent by the rise of third and fourth parties and by the division between the Conservative south-east of the country and the Labour strongholds in the north, in Scotland and in Wales. We do not want a repetition on the mainland of the position in Northern Ireland, where there is a permanent minority which, in the absence of electoral reform, would be insufficiently represented. Minorities in the north and south of the United Kingdom should be able to elect a fair quota of members.

The system of voting which is the most logical and the fairest is the single transferable vote. Under this system there must be more than two vacancies to be filled in each constituency. The voter marks the list of candidates in order of preference. Those with an overall majority, if there are any, are elected. If there are still seats to be filled, the votes are redistributed until the number of seats up for election are filled by candidates with the required quota of votes. Although this is the most logical system, as I say, I am not wholly enamoured of it. I am not convinced that votes cast without enthusiasm should count as much as those cast for candidates whom voters clearly want to see in Parliament. However, that is a somewhat metaphysical point.

This system has two practical drawbacks, apart from weakening the link between the Member and his or her constituency. It would beget some very large and heterogeneous constituencies. The most extreme case would be in the north of Scotland. My own constituency of Orkney and Shetland stretches for some 200 miles, farther than from London to York. To construct a constituency with any claim to return three Members of Parliament, the large landward areas of Caithness, Sutherland and Ross and Cromarty would have to be added. Even so, the size of the electorate would be far below the national average. With modern communications and wonders yet to come, mere size may to some extent be discounted. In many democracies – in the USA and some member countries of the EEC, for instance – constituencies are bigger. But I do not believe that television can be a satisfactory substitute for the flesh. Even if they do not come to meetings very much, I still hold that constituents should be given an opportunity to meet their candidates. But what is more serious is that large constituencies must mean that disparate communities would be yoked together. Caithness and Sutherland and Ross and Cromarty may have quite a lot in common with each other but not with Shetland. It is sometimes said that the single transferable vote suits cities. But to make three member constituencies around, say, Swansea, Dundee or Norwich, chunks of the neighbouring countryside, which is not necessarily homogeneous, would have to be added.

If we achieve electoral reform, it will be normal for several parties to have substantial representation in Parliament. It is sometimes forgotten that even now at least eight parties are represented in the House of Commons, but their representation is small compared with that of the Tory or Labour parties.

Before pursuing the question of how we might mend the present failings in our political system, we must look at what we mean by Parliament.

The Alliance is committed to 'devolution', as it has come to be called. I do not like the word, as it implies that power rests at Westminster, from which centre some may be graciously 'devolved'. I would rather begin by assuming that power should rest with the people who entrust it to their representatives to discharge the essential tasks of government. Once we accept, as I believe the Alliance does accept, that the Scots and the Welsh are nations, then we must accord them Parliaments which have all the normal powers of government, except for those that they delegate to the United Kingdom Government or the EEC. I find it difficult to see how, if the case for Scottish and Welsh self-government is accepted at all, any powers can be reserved to the UK Government except foreign affairs, defence and the wider issues of economic policy linked to a common currency and common trade policies. So when we consider Parliament we must think of three Parliaments and of a much restricted Westminster Parliament.

I am not convinced that the regions of England should be placed on a par with Scotland and Wales. Here I differ from what I take to be the official policy of both the Alliance and the Liberal Party (though there is a substantial minority in the SDP which agrees with me). I do not detect any national feeling in the north or west or Midlands of England comparable with that in Scotland or Wales. The demand for regional assemblies seems to be stimulated partly by a fear that if Scotland and Wales have Parliaments and executives, the regions of England will be at a disadvantage. Without assemblies of their own, they will not be able to milk the central government as effectively as their neighbours to the north and west.

This reveals what is, to me, a misunderstanding of what Scottish and Welsh self-government, leading to a type of federal system, is about. The object of giving responsibility to the Scots and Welsh is so that they can foster their own traditions, develop along the lines they choose, do something different from the English. If this is to be achieved, they must stop pulling at the apron strings of London. They must raise their own taxation and in the end, though this may have to come about gradually, cease to be dependent on the British Exchequer. In fact, the kind of self-government I advocate places responsibilities and obligations on the nation; it is not a method of creating a giant national lobby. If I were an Englishman, and particularly a Tory Englishman, I should be strongly in favour of Scottish self-government.

If we are to set up Parliaments for Scotland and Wales, what becomes of England? First, let me emphasize that we must fight against the tide which at every reform brings in more government and more bureaucrats. We have not yet recovered from the 'reform' of local government in 1972, which swept in a vast increase in staffs and expenditure. The Westminster Parliament cannot go on as it is now. Scottish representation must be reduced. The two most glaring mistakes of the Scottish Bills of 1976–7 and 1977–8 were the refusal to give powers of taxation to Scotland and the refusal to reduce the number of Scottish MPs. The reason for the latter decision was obvious – it would have damaged the Labour Party.

Scottish Members would be required at Westminster only when foreign affairs, defence and the larger issues of economic planning were discussed. I suggest that the ultimate solution must be that a delegation from the Scottish Parliament would meet with delegations from the English and Welsh Parliaments to discuss these matters, including the appointment of the Ministers concerned. My reason for suggesting this somewhat unusual proceeding, with its drastic deviation from our methods, is twofold. First, I do not believe that the usual methods appropriate to federations can be applied, partly because we already have a set of constituencies for the EEC and partly because of the disproportion in size between Scotland, Wales and England. Secondly, a fully-fledged federation would almost certainly invoke yet more government. If my scheme were adopted, the English Parliament, shorn of its Scottish and Welsh Members, could continue much as at present.

I am not convinced that the Alliance has faced the consequences of Scottish and Welsh self-government. It may well be right if it says that such radical changes as I suggest cannot be introduced at once. But, as over other issues which I regard as crucial to the test of whether we are a conservative or an initiating party, we must be clear what the issues are, and our short-term activities must not contradict our long-term policies.

The issue of Scottish and Welsh self-government raises another matter much in my mind. It may well be said not only that does neither country want what I recommend (because neither, if it considered them, would face the consequences) but also that Scotland and Wales are not cohesive countries in which self-rule could flourish. Undoubtedly in Scotland, outside the central belt, there is widespread suspicion of rule from Edinburgh or Glasgow. (As one of my constituents in Orkney put it, 'Who can think of anything more dreadful than being ruled by Glasgow trade unionists and Edinburgh lawyers?') In Northern Ireland we struggle to find a way by which a divided country can govern itself. In some local authorities we find the same division. North Wales is a different country from South Wales. There are even some who see a fatal division growing up between north and south England.

I do not accept that these fissiparous tendencies have gone so far as to threaten democratic government. I believe that the worst features of this tendency can be reversed. But, as with other somewhat crucial matters, the problem must be faced. If we are to decentralize power, we must either be sure that communities exist to assume it — that is to say, that there is in them both a common interest and fellow feelings — or we shall have to look for new and probably undemocratic forms of government. I supported the Bill to set up an Assembly in Northern Ireland because I am not prepared to abandon the hope that the Northern Irish can find enough common spirit to run their own affairs. But if the Assembly collapses, then we shall have to accept that the preconditions for democratic government do not exist in Northern Ireland by itself. The obvious alternative would be to absorb the Province within the general political structure of the UK. This measure might well protect the Roman Catholic minority from oppression, but it would surely have to be accompanied by some accommodation with Eire.

Neither democracy nor a free market can flourish without

common feelings and values. These can be manifested in different ways. The middle and working classes at the end of the last century had strong internal bonds. They differed from one another, recognized, sometimes resented, the differences. But they shared certain traditions and morals. At that time there was more conflict between the classes than, in many parts of the country, there is today. Common institutions, not mere instruments for pressure but independent and self-sufficient institutions holding certain standards in common, may be an alternative to classes — so, of course, may be a common religion. But I find it difficult to believe that British democracy can survive as a purely theoretical exercise. It must be founded on the desire to work together for a common good, on patriotism, if you like, on common traditions, on institutions which assert the legitimacy that they derive from the people and their country, not from the state. The Alliance must encourage such common feelings.

The electoral system will eventually, I hope, have to provide MPs for English, Scottish and Welsh Parliaments. Its task will be easier when that stage is reached. After the new allocation of seats that is under way, the British House of Commons will have 650 members — far more than any other legislative assembly. In addition, of course, we have the thousand or so peers, the European Parliament (neither European nor a Parliament, as someone has pointed out, but requiring support and attention now, while likely to become part of the governing process in the future). After taking into account local councils and subordinate bodies of all sorts, it is apparent that too many people are involved in the political arena even before we count the huge Civil Service. It would be highly undesirable to make the House of Commons any bigger. Indeed, it ought to be slimmed. Eventually, therefore, we should abolish the regions in Scotland. We should then equip Scotland and Wales with Parliaments, each of which would be smaller than the House of Commons but which in total would allow of slightly smaller constituencies and would reduce the size of the English Parliament.

But in the meantime how should the Alliance proceed? Neither a complete reorganization of constituencies to suit the single transferable vote nor self-government in Scotland and Wales could be brought into operation quickly. The first step must be to make the electoral system more responsive to the wishes of the electorate and to broaden the parties' too narrow political debate. I would therefore settle for the retention of single-Member constituencies for the British Parliament as long as it survives in its present form. But the House of Commons should also contain 'added Members' to balance the single-Member results. The number of constituencies would have to be reduced to make room for these 'added Members'. I suggest that the number might be reduced to, say, 550 seats, to which might be added eighty members. This system provokes paroxysms of horror, not least among electoral reformers. I do not myself like the extension of the parties' power which it involves. This could be mitigated by choosing the 'added Members' not from a list drawn up by the parties but from among the most successful of the unelected candidates of the party or parties which were under-represented in the constituencies by comparison with the overall percentage of the total vote. The alternative would be a second vote for the party list, as is the custom in West Germany. I stress that I would regard either innovation as temporary until the future government of the four elements of Britain had been decided.

The additional influence given to the established parties by these supplementary Members might be countered to some extent by the reform of the second chamber. Two of the questions which I raised earlier on in this chapter are, first, how do we assert the general interest and achieve in government a circumspection which takes on at the same time the productive capacity of the country and the demands made upon it, and, secondly, how do we strengthen representatives' ability to control the experts?

The second chamber should to some extent supply the answers to these questions. I have never been greatly impressed by the view that the main task of the Lords is revision. That much of the legislation that comes from the Commons badly needs revision I do not deny. But that is because there is so much of it and because the Commons handles it badly. Nor do I deny that good work is carried out by the Lords, but we hardly need 1,100 members to do it. It is more important, to my mind, that the Lords should be a watchdog. Between general elections the people can barely make their views known. With an all-powerful Parliament unfettered by a constitution and at present open to domination by a small minority of the electors, the dangers of damage to the general and lasting good of the country for some short-term gain by particular groups are serious.

I would therefore like to see a second chamber carrying some of the burden imposed by democratic authority but free from particular pressures or the dictates of the executive. A body of, say, 300 members, elected by single transferable vote in very large constituencies — say, thirty of ten members each — for a fixed period of, say, seven years might meet these requirements. I would hope that independent men and women, some with particular expertise, might serve on these conditions. Candidates with national reputations might well be elected, regardless of party support. Those elected would be largely free from the welfare demands made upon representatives of single-Member constituencies. The certainty of tenure for seven years should shield Members to some extent from the pressures of Governments and interest groups. The body should not have to meet often, its revising functions being delegated to committees. When Scotland and Wales get their own Parliaments it might still be useful to have a British second chamber. But it would surely have to be left to each of the three countries to decide whether or not to support the continuation of bicameral government.

The revising powers of the second chamber would remain, as would the present powers to delay. The only additional power which I contemplate would be a power to call for a referendum in certain circumstances. That there are difficulties over this I admit. Such a power should be reserved for major legislation only. How is that to be defined? The phrasing of the questions in a referendum is notoriously difficult. And there are other difficulties. But without such an appeal of last resort to the electorate, we would remain at the mercy of minority government. The extreme sensibility which was once shown (for example, by Asquith over the reform of the House of Lords) both to minorities and to the constitution has waned. Other countries do not find it impossible to handle referenda. Indeed, we have done so ourselves lately on at least two occasions. It might be possible to draw up some categories of legislation which were subject to referendum (and leave it to the Law Lords to interpret them). If then the Commons (that is, the government) and say a two-thirds majority of the second chamber disagreed, the matter might be put to the elector-ate.

As for reforms of the Commons to enable it to answer some of the questions raised earlier, an electoral system which more nearly represented the will of the people and a second chamber with greater authority would assist it.

The specialist committees have improved the scrutiny of govern-ment and in particular of government expenditure and I am in favour of retaining them — indeed, I suggested them long ago. But certain points in connection with the growth of the committee system need to be borne in mind.

I still believe that there is value in the English tradition by which the Commons is elected not to govern but to be a check upon government, to criticize and thwart government. There is a danger that a committee that constantly examines the work of a particular Ministry will become too involved with the work of that Ministry. The committee will come to sympathize with it and its Ministers. *Tout comprendre c'est tout pardonner.* But it is not the business of MPs to pardon. They may be much more effective critics if at arm's length from the executive. Over taxation, the very core of democratic control, it is particularly important that they should not sympathize with particular Ministries or, indeed, with the Government as a whole. It is all too easy for Ministries to smother criticism with a deluge of particular points and statistics. Richard Law, a Tory MP of the 1930s, told me once that when he pressed for more defence in general and more aircraft in particular, he constantly met with the objection that other commitments of the Government would not allow it. He conceived it his duty to reply, 'All I can tell you is that the first priority is to meet the threat from Hitler, though it is not my business to tell you what must be done to meet this. It must be met. More aircraft are essential. It is your business as Government to decide what must be sacrificed to do it. Not mine. If you are not capable of doing so, then go.' I believe he was right.

The committees, in any case, are confined to discussing whether policies have been implemented and efficiently carried out, not whether the machinery or policies of Government should be altered. They cannot therefore take the place of the general criticism of Government by back-benchers, which can only be ventilated in the Chamber. They must be careful that they do not weaken Parliament in its main task of checking the encroach-ment of Governments upon the citizen. But while the committee have their dangers and limitations, they have proved valuable in forcing Ministers into the open and in exposing slack administration. The Alliance should fortify them.

In spite of recent improvements, the consideration of expendi-ture and the assessment of revenue need to be brought nearer together. No business could survive which kept them on different balance-sheets. Indeed, we still have no national balance-sheet.

The business arrangements of the Commons too are still chaotic. Business is not known more than a week ahead at most. Govern-ments should lay down not a rigid programme but a guide to the timing of business at least a month ahead. The handling of Bills often means that early clauses are debated *ad nauseam*. A guillotine then falls, so that late clauses may not be discussed at all. Strong objections are always made to the imposition of a timetable on committees from the start of their consideration of a Bill. But the main objection, that a timetable infringes one of the last weapons of the Opposition, that of delay, has little validity. The Govern-ment gets its Bill by imposing the guillotine. Further, the use of delaying tactics means that too much of the time of committees is devoted to repetitions of general objections and too little to detailed consideration of Bills. I regret it, but I have come to the conclusion that an initial timetable covering the whole considera-tion of a Bill in committee is preferable to the present shambles.

It would also go some way towards bringing the public into closer contact with legislation if an opportunity were given to those interested in a particular Bill to hear it explained and to have an opportunity to ask questions about it. As with some private Bills, the Ministers should, in place of the vestigial first reading, appear before the public to justify their Bill and to hear suggestions or criticism. Some safeguards would have to be erected to prevent this process from being unduly prolonged, but, coupled with a timetable, I see no reason why the total time taken over Bills should be greatly increased. If the number of Bills were reduced, some further examination would indeed lead to better legislation.

If government, as Burke wrote, is 'a contrivance of human wisdom to satisfy human want' and has nothing God-given about it, we should be chary of extending its size or powers. It should be tailored to meet our needs and no more. It should respect the traditions and institutions of the country, particularly the common law and the whole conception of the rule of law. The public should be able to check and rebuke it. When we have a species of federal system in Britain, we shall require a written constitution, and with it perhaps should go a Bill of Rights. But until then, rather than graft a Bill of Rights on to our present constitution, I would rely more upon a strengthened second chamber, electoral reform, improvements in the procedures of the Commons and the removal of some activities from government control.

Managing the Economy

4

Short-Term Policies

The economic aim of the Alliance, on reaching a position of influence, will not differ significantly from that of most other parties — that is, to increase output and employment without inflation. The Alliance has already voiced its opinion that macro-economic policies can effect some reduction in unemployment without provoking undue inflation.

The elements of the short-term economic policy of the Alliance can be summarized as follows. It would increase public capital expenditure, abolish the National Insurance surcharge and cut VAT to 12.5 per cent. These and other minor adjustments would increase the public sector borrowing requirement (PSBR) by some £3—4 billion. It is calculated that they would create 85,000 jobs. The Alliance would also introduce certain other measures to create employment — for instance, an Environmental Improvement Programme. It would raise certain allowances (for example, child benefit), abolish the earnings rule for pensioners and give some further help to the poor, until an integrated tax/benefit system could be introduced. It would introduce an incomes policy with tax sanctions. It would intervene to keep down the exchange rate of the pound.

Before considering this or any policy, we must make some assessment of, or guess at, the state of the economy after the general election. There is little sign that the economy will be surging forward when the Government takes office, but it may be picking up. It seems to me likely that inflation, though at the time of writing it is still falling, will be stable or rising. The Government's control of the money supply has not been as strict as it intended. Energy prices may be rising again. Any signs of increased profitability will encourage unions to increase wage demands. However, inflation will probably still be constrained by unemployment and world conditions.

In the short term the Alliance will not have the chance greatly to change people's expectations, but the outlook may be slightly brighter in a year or so, and the advent of a responsible left party should in itself give some confidence to industry.

Let us consider first the management of demand. This is a sphere in which the same policies apply to both the short and the long term. Mrs Thatcher's Government made a serious error when it raised VAT and granted large increases in the pay of public servants during its first year of office. These measures were inconsistent with the Government's long-term aims. Once again the lesson was rubbed home that parties should not make large commitments at a general election; whether that lesson will ever be learned is a different matter.

One of the first tasks of the Alliance should be to clarify its attitude to the monetarists versus Keynesians row. In its simplest terms the disagreement is about what happens if Governments attempt to increase output and employment by spending more. The monetarists argue that higher public expenditure designed to increase employment can only do so, if at all, in the short term. In the long term such an increase decreases the efficiency of labour, at best results in creating some new jobs at the expense of losing existing ones and ends up by raising prices. Inflation is caused by the debasement of the currency — however currency is defined. If you increase the quantity of money, you decrease its value. This is obviously true, other things being equal. It is also true that Mr Jenkins and Mr Healey were monetarists when at the Exchequer, in that they sought to control the money supply. It is also true, as Friedman among others has pointed out, that the controversy about monetarism is separate from the controversy about state control of industry or socialism in general. Several socialist political economists and several communist governments have been monetarists. Friedman and his associates are also right in saying that governments must calculate in money and not in 'real' terms, otherwise inflation becomes endemic and progressive. All governments are tempted to inflate, and few resist the temptation. Inflation is part of the age-old technique of *panem et circenses*, the beguiling of the electorate, the pandering to powerful interests and the distraction from tackling the causes of economic failure. It has been the downfall of several empires.

But the monetarists seem to me to ignore the conditions in which we live. Until these have been adjusted, indeed radically altered, their analysis needs revision. The motives of the huge public sector are not those of people or organizations which spend their own money. The divorce between the suppliers and spenders of wealth is a major factor in today's economy. An increase in prices will not necessarily make a public authority economize. It will demand more money, to be supplied directly or indirectly through taxation. The power of certain trade unions, restrictive practices, the multitude of regulations to be obeyed, the interests of managements social obligations and the imperfections of capital and labour markets all present obstacles to the operation of monetarism. For instance, it is said that if the Government invests, it can do so only by appropriating funds which would otherwise be available for private and probably more lucrative and efficient investment. But this is not so. In today's world there are fields in which if the Government does not invest, no one will. Investment in some of these fields — for instance, in new technologies over the long term or in basic needs now publicly controlled — may well be necessary.

The Keynesians, to put their case crudely, argue that where there are unused resources or an excess of savings over investment, it is sensible for the Government to undertake some investment and to seek to bring the economy into better balance by releasing some purchasing power. The difficulty here is that those who preach Keynesianism often equate any public expenditure on capital projects with investment. Governments have constantly pumped the taxpayers' money into projects which have a low commercial value, if they have any at all. This is not investment. It may give temporary employment, but it produces no assets capable of yielding long-term wealth nor, indeed, long-term employment. Further, though Keynes certainly gave due weight to the obstructions in the British economy which prevented macro-measures from taking effect and distorted investment, the economy has become even stickier since his day. Another feature of our economy which must be kept in mind is the growth of pension and insurance funds and their effects, as set out by Mr John Plender in his book *That's the Way the Money Goes.** (I refer to these in more detail in the next chapter.)

In short, both monetarists and Keynesians tend to neglect the circumstances of the modern world. To these the Alliance must pay attention. Most of our so-called economic problems are political problems. The actions of the trade unions, for instance, which may delay or totally frustrate the intentions of a Chancellor of the Exchequer, are the products of political decisions. The importance that we attach to relief from unemployment, for example, as against perhaps extra productivity or a reduction in inflation, is a political judgement.

Since I have been in Parliament no incoming Government has been prepared for office. They all complain of the mess which they have inherited. I can remember that it was said that when Churchill took over in 1951 so appalling was the confusion inherited from the late Labour Government that he was advised not to take office until the books had been audited. Of course, if such advice was tendered, he ignored it. However great the hardship of office, few refuse it — certainly not Churchill. Nor indeed was the legacy of that Government particularly flawed.

Not only does each new Government complain of its inheritance, but also each seems to be caught unaware of the present in which it is living. The party manifestos get longer; the researchers proliferate; but a Government finds that the world is on the move and will not hold back while it drafts the Bills which its promises require. To make matters worse, not only are all Governments distracted by the pressing needs of the moment, particularly the economic moment, but they appear to get entrapped in a whole quiverful of measures which their civil servants consider essential. They also seem oblivious to the seeds already sown and the forces already fermenting. They are apt to meet problems which are already passing. When the economy has already turned upwards they apply more stimulants without heeding the dangers of inflation.

* London: André Deutsch, 1982.

The Alliance, if it is in a position to influence government in the near future, will put the reduction of unemployment at the top of its politico-economic policies. It will meet not only the general objection that you cannot spend your way out of a depression, as useful employment is not in the gift of Governments, but also the further difficulty that unemployment differs very considerably from district to district and is due partly to causes such as the inflexibility of the economy which will take time to cure. How can we devise a policy which will not increase inflation and will be appropriate to the different areas of Britain? (In the long term, of course, the problems of different areas require structional change.)

In the macro-economic sphere the package suggested by Mr Roy Jenkins at the Hillhead by-election seems to me to offer the right sort of balance. He proposed an increase in the PSBR of the order of £3 billion, to be used largely for public works, and the reduction of taxes on employment, as set out at the beginning of this chapter. Some of these proposals are being adopted by the present Chancellor of the Exchequer, and he will no doubt have moved further in Mr Jenkins's direction by the time of the general election. Nevertheless, some stimulation of demand, as suggested by Mr Jenkins, will probably still be necessary and will probably be achieved without adding much to inflation.

Even according to the most optimistic forecasts, however, the additional expenditure proposed by the Alliance will not reduce unemployment by more than half a million within, say, two years. Where does the Alliance stand on the issue of how the expansion in the economy is to be started? It would deny, I take it, that expansion will come of itself. It would maintain that Governments can assist recovery. Yet the assistance that it proposes is moderate, and its effects will be equally moderate. Is this pump-priming? Having injected a degree of extra demand into the economy, does the Alliance believe that it will snowball? Or are its proposals designed to mitigate the slump until the upturn in the economy cycle takes over? My own view is that Governments have some, but a limited, ability to create employment — that is, they can do so temporarily and in defined areas such as essential public works. That snarling question 'How does economic expansion start?', so often asked of the Government by its critics and implying that the

Government itself must start it or stand condemned as a collection of Micawbers, seems to me slightly unfair. Slumps end. No one knows exactly why, but they do end, and recovery is usually worldwide. Individual governments may sponsor international action; they may accelerate or impede recovery in their own countries, but off their own bat they can seldom, if ever, ignite the process. It is possible that the new technology will spark off a fresh flare-up, just as the inventions of the late eighteenth century fuelled nineteenth-century expansion. At present the policy must be to hold the fort, so to speak, to back up tendencies to expansion until we can greatly improve the performance of the economy. I believe that although an extra half-million jobs is much to be welcomed, the Alliance should not fall victim to the delusion that by itself, and immediately, it will be able to conquer unemployment.

To turn to the management of supply: the capacity of our economy to produce has been curtailed. Why? Not, I suggest, solely because of a failure of demand. At some levels — the retail trade, for example — there is a reasonably high demand. And in 1983 demand in general is rising. It is because the incentives for production are inadequate. A high proportion of the earnings of producers are transferred by the Government (through transfer payments) to others (pensioners, clients of the welfare services and others). The incentives to increase production are of various sorts: the likely return on capital and exertion, some assurances that profits will continue to be earned (and not taxed to extinction), the future of world trade, common effort in industry. The main thrust of the economic policy of the Alliance must be to promote more efficient production of goods for which there is a market — either a national or an international market or both.

The Alliance should look favourably on four suggestions which would operate chiefly on the supply side of the economy. One of these appears in the appendix, 'A Financial and Economic Scheme', attached to the note of dissent to the Kilbrandon Report* by Lord Crowther-Hunt and Professor Peacock. With the details of

---

* *The Report of the Kilbrandon Commission on the Constitution*, Cmnd 5460, London: HMSO, 1973.

this appendix I am not concerned. Its planning proposals seem to be doubtfully feasible. But its general idea, I am sure, is right — that is, that we should build up from local needs and possibilities. Thus instead of trying to find a policy suitable for, Bournemouth, Sunderland and Shetland, we should make an estimate of the investment which could usefully be achieved by each area in, say, three years and both tailor national policies to meet these requirements and also specifically direct investment to likely projects.

The next two suggestions which seem to me to be valuable come from articles published in the *Financial Times* in February 1982. The first, by Professor Layard,* argues that by concentrating state aid, better and cheaper results could be achieved than by giving across-the-board help (for example, by cutting the national insurance surcharge). Professor Layard estimated that, at the time he was writing, to offer a subsidy of £70 a week for a year for all increases in employment over the previous year would cost the Exchequer about the same (in gross terms) as a cut in the national insurance surcharge of £3 a week. The Professor would, however, like to see the aid 'targeted' on the long-term unemployed. In the same article he suggests a plan for those not absorbed by industry, under which they would be employed, for very little more than their unemployment pay, on schemes directed towards environmental improvement. I am rather against 'tailored' or 'targeted' assistance of this sort as a long-term policy, believing that in most spheres of activity the market is the best regulator. But the market is so distorted, centralization so deeply ingrained, the difference in prosperity between different areas of the country so acute, that this type of discrimination seems at present to be inevitable.

The second suggestion comes from Mr Samuel Brittan,† who points out that capital has been quite ridiculously subsidized. The fashion being for technology, Governments have poured money into capital allowances while penalizing the employment of men and women. According to the figures he quotes, an employer has to pay £82 a week to provide a net wage of £50. Mr Brittan proposes a reduction both in the tax allowances and subsidies for capital and in the taxes on labour. He also points out that employ-

* 'The cheapest way to get more jobs', 24 February.
† 'A new look at productivity', 25 February.

ment protection and redundancy legislation deters possible employers from taking on labour. The fact that capital has been
heavily subsidized does not mean that there has been too much
investment in Britain. But the lack of investment which has handi-
capped some of our industries has been due to the poor return on
it and to the deflection of savings to wasteful projects.

Finally, there is the old Liberal Party policy of varying taxation
such as the employers' insurance premiums between areas, so that
those with high unemployment pay less.

These schemes start from the realities of life in the different
regions, industries and age groups of Britain. They do not begin with
some all-embracing plan which ignores the real world. According
to their protagonists, they would not greatly increase the PSBR.
If they were initiated, some of the present rather ineffective assistance to special areas could be repealed. There are three major
faults of the present legislation that is designed to help areas of
high unemployment. First, it is 'handed down' from the centre.
Not only does this mean that it is too generalized and theoretical;
it also means that the schemes are centrally controlled and the
beneficiaries tend to be branch factories of centrally – or foreign
– controlled companies. Secondly, the legislation does not ensure
that a higher proportion of the wealth generated remains in the
regions which need it. Under the present schemes much of the
money pumped into outlying and under-employed regions finds
its way back to the more prosperous areas, as was pointed out to
me long since by Professor Paish. Further, as with so much of our
legislation, that designed to help the backward areas is chaotic. I
need only cite two examples from my own constituency. There
are said to be forty schemes, British and EEC, under which crofters
can claim aid. The oil companies, which are hardly among our
most impoverished institutions, receive development grants for
doing what they would do in any case – that is, bringing North
Sea oil ashore in my constituency. Of course, with the other hand
the Government is exacting heavy taxes from them. The third
fault of the present policies is a structural one. They do nothing
to discourage the over-centralization of decision-making that is
prevalent throughout our political economy. This fault can be
completely cured only in the longer term, but a shift of policy

along the lines I have sketched above could be initiated at once.

I can see no practical difficulty raised by the geography or industry of Britain that should stand in the way of such a change in policy. I can see every reason why it should appeal to the Alliance. All the suggestions emanate from sources which are sympathetic to the Alliance. They are also in accord with Green Paper No. 1* and the proposals of the Tawney Society.

The main instruments at hand for examining which local projects can usefully be backed so as to avoid pouring money down unproductive drains are the ICFC, which has local offices, and the public development agencies, such as the Highlands and Islands Development Board. Local authorities should also be consulted. It must be emphasized, however, that local authorities, as at present constituted, are not ideal for the task of deciding about local development for the reasons examined in chapter 2. What I would urge is that the Alliance should at once make contact with local entrepreneurs, bankers and so on with a view to having some schemes ready when it takes office. The nature of its membership, particularly that of the SDP, containing a high proportion of skilled people, should make this easy. Local associations should be given the task of examining the resources and needs of their neighbourhoods — a task they would welcome and which would engage them in constructive work in a way that I believe should be encouraged. While we are breaking the mould we must flout the traditional view that political activity must be confined to working for or at elections.

The Alliance believes that a more generous supply of money and some increase in the PSBR would require an incomes policy if inflation were to be contained. Indeed, a permanent, legally enforceable incomes policy was the distinctive feature of the economic policy of the Liberal Party and at one time seemed to have been taken on by the SDP. Exactly what form of incomes policy the Alliance now favours is not as clear, but certainly it is committed to an incomes policy of sorts.

Why should an incomes policy be necessary? The main argument for such a policy is that if the economy is inflated, even by the fairly modest amount proposed by Mr Jenkins, the extra

* *Towards Full Employment: A Commonsense Approach to Economic Policy.*

money will go to raise wages and prices and not to create more jobs. In containing wage and salary rises by limiting them to a maximum each year, the Alliance hopes that the extra money which it intends to make available will not lead solely to higher wages, prices and an increased flow of imports. The argument, in fact, assumes that the monetarists are right. The policy also implicitly accepts that a free, liberal democracy will not work. It is argued, on the one hand, that the market is too imperfect to do the job of containing prices and, on the other, that there is no sense of common purpose sufficient to take its place. Those who advocate an incomes policy are implicitly agreeing with the view that Britain is fragmented and at the mercy of the sort of free-for-all that Hobbes feared. Every trade union must be aware that if it and all other unions obtain higher pay without increased productivity, this can lead only to inflation and unemployment. This has been happening and, until recently, happening at a growing pace. Between 1974 and 1979 the gross domestic product rose in money terms by nearly 129 per cent. Of this rise roughly 10 per cent was due to an increase in output and 119 per cent to inflation. But each trade union and similar body is afraid that if it abates its claim, its colleagues will steal a march on it. This is a consequence of lack of common trust. Once again we see that our troubles are moral or political. Further, until recently Governments calculated in 'real' terms and so felt bound to increase money expenditure to catch up with inflation (a tail-chasing exercise for which Keynes, somewhat unjustly, has been blamed). The position has been aggravated by indexation, hire purchase and other built-in obligations which individuals find calculated in rising money prices. So, the argument runs, we must impose order on anarchy by means of an incomes policy.

All incomes policies, as opposed to new ways of negotiating wages and salaries, have three points in common: they depend upon the permissible increase (or, in theory, possible decrease) for wages and salaries being fixed at regular intervals (usually annually); they require machinery for imposing the policy and making the necessary interpretations and exceptions; and they demand that some allowance must be made for the circumstances of different bodies of workers when the policy is enacted. There are many other refinements and requirements in the various incomes policies which have been suggested, but even these three basic requirements need time to implement, so if an incomes policy is to be a short-term instrument, the Alliance will have to keep it as simple as possible. If the Alliance is to impose an incomes policy at all, there seems to me much to be said for a straightforward freeze of all wages and salaries above, say, £7,000 a year. Under £7,000 a year a flat maximum increase of, say, £500 might be sanctioned. Of course, this would be unfair, especially as between those with very valuable perks and payments in kind and those with few or none. But note that I propose a flat rate rather than a percentage increase, so that the lowest-paid would benefit more.

The justification for a short-term incomes policy is that it would give the Government time to institute long-term structural reform while at the same time increasing employment and holding down inflation, thereby generating confidence. The arguments against it are that even in the short term it would be illiberal and unjust, that it would make the economy even less flexible and resilient, that behind it claims would build up which would lead to an even more violent explosion of wage-based inflation when it was removed. The implication is that so far from curbing expectations of inflation, an incomes policy might fuel them. (Though I am aware that there is a school of thought which denies that increases in wages cause inflation, high wages unjustified by increases in productivity must, directly or indirectly, contribute to unemployment and inflation.) It would acknowledge the threat of inflation and yet give no assurance that it would be removed; it would only be postponed. There would then be a need to get in before the ban on wage increase and a stirring of ambitions to start up again when the ban was lifted.

To my mind no liberal can welcome a statutory incomes policy of any sort, long-term or short-term. It shows that common feelings, the bonds of a liberal society have collapsed. It renounces the market and one important liberty, the liberty of everyone to sell his labour. It is indeed an attempt to drive the economy with one foot on the accelerator and the other on the brake. Some of the objections to it will be removed, however, if two considerations are borne in mind. First, the Government as employer is bound to have an incomes policy for the public sector. While the public sector remains so large, this must affect incomes in the private sector. Secondly, to make the structural changes which Britain needs will be a Herculean task, justifying some temporary suspension of normal procedures, as in time of war. If the time gained by an incomes policy is used to make, or at least to start, these structural changes, then expectations may be altered. There is one other matter that is crucial to the adoption of such a policy. I shall argue when discussing the social services (see chapter 6) that the great need is to raise the lower incomes and unscramble the intolerable complication of the present services. If we are to have an incomes policy, it should be a first step in that direction. (Hence my recommendation that instead of a percentage increase a flat rate should be imposed.) It should not freeze incomes at their present levels. The very highest incomes in the public service (for example, the Civil List) might actually be reduced. Senior civil servants who take on to lucrative jobs outside the Civil Service should forfeit part or all of their indexed pensions. Such measures would at least set an example. Very high salaries in the private sector should be taxed at rates of up to 90 per cent. No increases should be allowed in salaries over £7,000 a year, as I have suggested, but rather large increases should be allowed at the bottom of the scale. If the wages freeze were to be maintained for any length of time, it would have to be accompanied by a freeze on incomes of all kinds, such as dividends and rent. There would also probably have to be a freeze on prices. The expense and difficulty of setting this in train would be enormous, the results by no means clearly predictable. I would myself embark on it only as a last resort. But the Alliance seems committed to an incomes policy of some sort, and I would prefer a short-term freeze to a permanent statutory policy.

When we come to consider, in chapter 5, the long-term economic policies which the Alliance should pursue, these to my mind are very largely structural and spill over into changes in industrial relations, the ownership of industry and political reforms. But before coming to these we must examine further the arguments for and against permanent incomes policies. For if the Alliance is involved in government, it presumably intends, at an early stage in the new Parliament, to draft legislation for a long-term incomes policy.

The Gang of Four and the Liberal leadership have all come out in favour of one. Dr Owen in his book *Face the Future* writes bluntly: 'The history of the last thirty-five years suggests that full employment, reasonable price stability and free collective bargaining are mutually incompatible' (p. 147). The type of policy which the Alliance seems most to favour is that propounded by Professor Layard, under which some norm would be established for pay increases. Employers would not be forbidden to break the norm, but if they did so, they would be heavily taxed. The scheme has considerable refinements, which I do not propose to set out in detail; the tax levied on firms that broke the norm would, for instance, be returned to industry. Professor Layard's proposals, if we are to have such a policy at all, are rather attractive.

But while I admit the temptation of falling back on an incomes policy after the constant failure to achieve growth with any degree of price stability, the proposals seem to me to have conclusive drawbacks. The first is that they constitute a surrender. They are an admission that the trade unions will never take a wider view. They throw in the sponge before structural change has been attempted. Even if this surrender is considered inevitable, it will not be a surrender with honour, nor is it likely to lead to fruitful peace. Why should the employer be penalized? It is improbable that in most cases in which wages above the norm are paid the fault will be his. The sanction would seem to me to be yet another whip laid across the back of the very people who are penalized at present and who ought to be encouraged. The fault of paying high wages, if it is a fault, is more likely to be due to union pressure than to an employer's profligacy. Punitive taxation would seem to be a further drawback to creating more jobs. It would apply a further and a damaging brake on mobility in the economy, not temporarily but permanently. It would not, I would have thought, be easily accepted by the trade unions and would encourage the development of an even more flourishing black economy. Also, as Professor Ball has pointed out, 'A permanent incomes policy [would] be the thin end of a very large wedge — a high degree of centralization in the allocation of economic resources.'* It would accentuate the central dictatorship of the economy to which many SDP supporters are opposed. The central government decisions on which the norm would be based would presuppose that the authorities could choose a certain level of output and employment and achieve it through a combination of fiscal, monetary and incomes policies. I doubt if this is possible.

Another suggestion that has aroused much interest in the SDP is that of Professor Meade. He writes that 'an acceptable solution . . . cannot be found through any centralized system of setting rates of pay.'† He therefore rejects the type of policy which limits increases to a percentage of current salaries, wages or incomes. Such policies freeze the economy in its present unsatisfactory state. They also mean that those with large salaries get substantial monetary increases and those on low salaries small ones and that everyone demands the maximum allowable. As opposed to a scheme such as Professor Layard's, under which the sanction is extra tax, Professor Meade would allow free bargaining. If no agreement were reached within thirty days, the parties would have to go to arbitration. But the arbitration tribunal would have only two choices: to enforce either the last offer by the employer or the last demand by the workers. In coming to its decision it would have regard to one criterion only: which demand will promote employment? This is an ingenious device first suggested in America. Those negotiating for the workers would know that if they pitched their claims too high, so that businesses would become unprofitable and workers would have to be laid off, they would be turned down. Equally, an employer who could pay more and expand his business would fail before the tribunal if he offered too little. Compromise, which at present is the usual end of such negotiations, would be impossible.

The scheme, as I say, is ingenious; but it seems to me to have two drawbacks. First, I do not see how it would help in the public sector. Many nationalized industries are reducing their work forces and are unprofitable already. No increase of pay, however small,

* R.J. Ball, *Money and Employment*, London: Macmillan, 1982, p. 204.
† J.E. Meade, *Stagflation*, vol. 1, *Wage-Fixing*, London: Allen and Unwin, 1982, p. 108.

will boost employment. Therefore, at present at least, the tribunal would be bound to find for an employer who offered nothing. (Incidentally, I am not sure whether in cases in which a reduction in wages would lead to more employment the tribunal would be bound to find for an employer seeking to enforce such a reduction.) Professor Meade's formula would not, I would have thought, have been much help in the disputes over nurses' pay or the claim of the Associated Society of Locomotive Engineers and Firemen. Secondly, I do not foresee that the work force would be content if, having had the employer's offer enforced, the company in question perhaps took on very few new employees but greatly increased its profits and the emoluments of its directors. I am not sure whether Professor Meade envisages bargaining for increases covering a whole industry and carried on by the trade union concerned or whether there would be plant bargaining. If the former, then the criterion by which the tribunal would have to Work would be the effect on employment over the whole industry, even if some firms would be forced to lay off workers as a result.

In the great majority of cases it is probable that the arbitrator would find for the employer. Professor Meade expects his method of pay fixing to be operated when the economy is gradually expanding. But even then the question behind many pay disputes will not necessarily be how to expand employment but how to remain competitive. Particularly at a time when technology is cutting the demand for some types of labour, an award of higher wages will seldom, I would have thought, lead to more employment. There is also the stickiness of the supply of labour. Even though companies could expand, a shortage of skilled labour might prevent this. Presumably in such circumstances the arbitrator would be unable to recommend a rise in wages.

Like other economists, Professor Meade proposes that we should aim at a steady increase in the money supply and also stresses the importance of encouraging the mobility of labour by curbing unnecessary apprenticeship requirements, increasing the number of houses available for letting and providing more information about jobs available. All these proposals would, I hope, be included in Alliance policy. But before turning to further

conclusions about an incomes policy, we should look at the structure of industry, for if it can be reformed, perhaps a statutory
incomes policy need not form part of the longer economic strategy.

I cannot reconcile myself to accepting for all time that because
money ('hot' money, as it is called) leaves the City of London,
British industry should have to pay higher interest rates. High
interest rates are widely canvassed as one of the worst handicaps
of the British economy. The argument for reducing public borrowing is that only by so doing can interest rates be kept down. Any
attempt to hold them down below the market rate for capital, it
is said, can only result in inflation and the misapplication of
resources. Yet when interest rates are raised to 'protect the pound'
we do not hear an outcry from the City at this interference with
the 'natural' rate. It cannot be beyond the wit of man to devise a
system by which industry and trade are liberated from these blows
from the money market. In the autumn of 1982, after interest
rates had fallen, the production of wealth was beginning to benefit
from the fall and business had done nothing to deserve punish-
ment, we were threatened with higher rates again, owing to
a flight of capital from London.

I do not pretend to know how this folly can be avoided, but I
do know that the present system is nonsense. However, to change
it will take time. In the meantime, should the Alliance recommend
either a deliberate reduction in interest rates — risking some
inflation — or differential rates for different classes of business?
I am not expert enough to know which expedient is to be recommended, but as temporary measures they do not seem to me beyond
the pale.

As for the exchange rate, the SDP policy-makers have suggested
some method by which it could be reduced to the benefit of
exports. About the feasibility of their proposals, again, I am not
competent to pronounce. I am somewhat chary, however, about
the efficacy of competitive devaluations or the advisability of
Britain's playing the lead in blocking world trade, from which she
gains so much. If we must indulge in protection, either because we
are inefficient or because we demand too much in wages or are
faced with 'unfair' competition, then I would favour some direct

measure aimed at specific goods by way of tariff or quota. The arguments against traffic and quotas are well known and compelling. Most of the excuses for these measures involve accepting faults such as over-manning and restrictive practices which should be abolished. Nevertheless, protection is one of those measures — like an incomes policy — which crop up with predictable regularity as Britain is faced with the social consequences of her inability to compete.

Tariffs have been advocated from time to time by members of the Department of Applied Economics at Cambridge. Their argument is really the 'infant industries' case over again. British industry, they maintain, has been unprofitable and uncompetitive, especially where exports are concerned. It will not undertake the necessary investment and reorganization unless it can see profitable markets for its products. Cutting taxes and grants or increasing government expenditure will not by themselves be enough. Therefore, foreign goods must be excluded. In fact, tariffs are alternatives to reducing the value of the pound. Devaluations do not offer much benefit for long and cannot be continuously repeated.

I find the arguments unconvincing, even as part of a medium-term economic policy. Some British industry is becoming highly competitive. Tariffs, I fear, would only restore it to its complacent state. They might protect the inefficient for a while, but only at the expense of the efficient and the country as a whole. And at a time when it is necessary to promote international co-operation in order to end the recession their effects on trade and international opinion would be peculiarly damaging.

But is there another case for tariffs in the short term? There would certainly be no such case were we to set about the structural changes that are essential to the way in which we run our affairs. The closest approximation to a case for tariffs is the reasoning put to me by Dr John Murray. He, although himself a convinced free-trader, points out that the British economic equation can be brought back into equilibrium, with an increase in employment, only if something 'gives'. If it is impossible to reduce wages further at present (for various reasons, including the level of unemployment pay that is available), impossible to increase output per unit of production, impossible indeed to increase efficiency in the short run, then imports may have to be controlled temporarily. This reasoning stems from the same foreboding as leads its exponents to favour an incomes policy — that is to say, the fear that the sort of inflation required to boost employment at home will only lead to an increase in imports. My fear is that once we indulge in tariffs, there will be pressure to retain and extend them. There is also the danger of retaliation, and we have obligations particularly within the EEC. Tariffs seem more addictive and more reprehensible than an incomes policy. But I accept that if our obligations allow, there may be a case for short sharp protection for certain industries, just as there may be a case for a temporary incomes policy.

Other measures to be initiated as soon as the Alliance has influence are a commitment to a low but steady increase in the money supply, as advocated by Professor Meade, and the simplification of the tax system. Few steps other than drastic cuts in tax rates could do more to help small businesses.

I do not believe that drastic cuts in taxation will be possible at once, and they should not be promised. The endless fiddling with taxation and the constant anxiety of all Chancellors to plug all possible escape routes for taxpayers I regard as major handicaps to business. As with the social services, the complication of taxation is insupportable. It also leads to the diversion of much effort, and many of our best brains, into the accounting profession. There are, I believe, over ten times as many accountants in Britain as in West Germany — a difference which may account for some part of the latter's commercial success.

My own view is that the difficulty of handling the finance of the public sector is a major cause of our economic troubles. This difficulty arises both from the size of the public sector and from the lack of any principle in paying for it. With neither of these can much be done in the first year or so of a new Government. In the long run the policies of the Alliance with respect to this sector will be an important element in its success or failure. Its immediate actions must point towards long-term objectives.

As soon as possible the Alliance should recast the Budget. The confusion over capital and income in the national accounts has meant that justifiable public investment has been cut. It is easier for public authorities to cut investment than to prune current expenditure, especially when current cuts affect salaries, wages and staff numbers.

Let me reiterate that I am not convinced that our poor economic performance is due solely to lack of money for capital projects. Much of the money nominally invested does not go to create investment at all. It leads to a waste of resources, which are diverted either to projects which can never pay and, if undertaken at all, should come under the heading of welfare or social services, or it is under-used. It is true that we have recently invested less in industry than have our competitors and true too that the British worker has less horsepower to his elbow than his American or Japanese counterpart. This is not, however, for lack of public money, which is poured out on to the sands of political expediency and restrictive practices.

Nevertheless, public capital expenditure which goes to useful or profitable purposes need not be inflationary and should be separated, from the point of view of the Budget and the PSBR, from current public expenditure. Much of it, essential if production is to rise, is as desirable as useful private investment. An increase in public expenditure on sewers and some of the capital needs of transport might not give directly much extra employment but should be included in the first Budget package. When we come to public-sector investment in housing and the nationalized industries, the Alliance must be clear about its long-term policies before deciding how to handle these. Here I need mention only some broad conclusions that I have reached. The Alliance should encourage house ownership and should turn more and more council houses over to owner-occupation and housing co-operatives. As to the nationalized industries, the process of decentralization should continue, though preferably responsibility should be handed over to co-operatives and other forms of employee control. Even those which remain under the present form of state control should be told to raise as much capital as they can on the market. The short-term tactics of the first Budget should not run counter to these longer-term aims.

Another point to be borne in mind is Keynes's conclusion that to raise employment an increase in demand must be supplemented by ad hoc measures. The commissioning of public works was proposed by Keynes after the First World War and was prominent among the suggestions of the Liberal Yellow Book. Today I believe Keynes would approve the 'targeting' of a high proportion of such works on areas of particularly high unemployment. It has again and again been pointed out that the stickiness of our economy over housing and many other disincentives to movement prevent macro-economic measures from having their full effect. This stickiness, which is in itself a cause of unemployment, should be reduced, but in the meantime areas of high unemployment should be given priority with respect to public works. So any injection of money into the nationalized industries that is aimed at increasing house building should be achieved by reviving the scheme initiated by Peter Walker, for which some preliminary planning presumably still exists, and by assisting those who are prepared to acquire or to build their own houses, whether as individuals or co-operatively.

As for assistance to capital projects, the method of providing investment for industry must be discussed when we turn to the longer term. I have long argued that there seems to be no adequate way of offering to local savers opportunities for investing in the equity of local firms. But in the first year or so of any Government in which the Alliance has influence use will have to be made of existing channels. These fall under three heads: direct government investment, investment through an agency and encouragement (say, by means of tax relief) to investment from private sources. At first sight it may seem that the second of these methods, investment through existing agencies, would be the best. Such agencies are in being and have some experience in the provision of capital to industry. But the drawbacks are threefold. First, in the long term new methods of investment must be found, so it would be undesirable to raise existing organizations' hopes of a long lease. Secondly, such organizations have a patchy record. Thirdly, with some exceptions — for instance, the Highlands and Islands Development Board — they tend to be London-orientated, while investment is needed which will not only provide jobs but will also stimulate enterprise elsewhere. (Even the HIDB seems to favour the accountant as against the entrepreneur. It is currently advertising for two accountants for its staff in Orkney.) Nevertheless, some use could be made of agencies, particularly those which are not under the control of the Government, such as the ICFC. At present the ICFC gets its funds from the banks. It might object to being involved with the Government. It seems to me, however, that it is the instrument most readily to hand, other than the Department of Industry itself, by which some public investment might be made in private industry. It has already to some extent devolved its decision-making and could no doubt do so further. Lord Seebohm and Lord Caldecote have looked favourably on management buy-outs, job-ownership companies and producer co-operatives, which, in the longer run, the Alliance should strenuously encourage.

In the short term I doubt if the Alliance can dramatically change the economic outlook. I suspect that by the next election the Government will be easing the economic squeeze on the economy in general. As I have already said, it has not altered the economic balance of the country. The percentage of GDP taken by the Exchequer is higher than ever. The nationalized industries have not lacked subsidies. The Alliance can lean rather more heavily on measures which, I suspect, the Chancellor will be already embracing. It can increase the PSBR, which, by historical comparisons, is low. It can initiate the measures suggested above. But the real test will be whether it can introduce some hope and competence and initiate long-term policies which will break the mould which has constricted our economic expansion for so long.

5

The Long View

Economists rightly stress the importance of expectations. There can be several views about the nature of the expectations cherished by most people and even more argument about whether they are justified and whether Governments should assist in their realization. I find that four categories of expectation can be identified: those of the bureaucrats, the leaders of big business and the trade unions; those of people lower down the hierarchies of business and the Civil Service and the self-employed, including farmers and fishermen; those of the groups interested in nuclear disarmament, ecology, the simple life and so on; and those of Marxists. The common features of the expectations of the first three is that although they remain high, no one is very certain that they will be attained. They are fuelled by bureaucratic attitudes and advertising. They are subject to changing fashions.

When it comes to the attainment of expectations, the first group looks to the success of its organizations in lobbying or bullying the Government to further its particular interests. It is concerned with prestige, security, status, and looks largely for perks and hand-outs to maintain and raise its standard of life. Its expectations have been, for instance, greatly enhanced by indexed pensions. On the whole, it expects its trade unions (and under this heading I include such bodies as the English Bar Council) to protect its interests successfully, even at the expense of the general good. But it is pessimistic about achieving this through its own efforts to increase its efficiency or enhance its popularity in the face of what it sees as threats from a changing world, and it looks to the Government to provide. The expectations of this

group can be seen in the pronouncements of all kinds of organization, from the CBI, the public and nationalized companies,
through to the National Union of Mineworkers, the National
Union of Public Employees, the Civil Service and so on.

The second group also looks for the Government's support but
is not as sanguine about getting it, fearing that the enthusiasm of
the Government for, say, agriculture or small businesses may be a
passing phase, apt to be jettisoned, in any case inadequate to meet
the long-term aspirations of those affected.

The third group too looks for salvation through Governments
but, unlike the first, does not feel satisfied with the predominant
attitudes of Governments since the war. Certainly, it makes full
use of the welfare services and is by no means the party of small
government, but it is worried by what it considers the dangerous
policies of the Establishment over such developments as nuclear
power and growth.

In some ways the rosiest expectations are those of the Marxists,
who believe that history is on their side. They are the ultimate
prophets of government and the bureaucracy.

There remains the possibility of a further group or a change in
the expectations of the first two groups. The current popularity
of the Tory Government, as I write, may be due not only to the
disintegration of the Labour Party or to the Falklands adventure
but also to the supposition that Tory economic policies will work.
The expectations of the first three groups that I have mentioned
include inflation. It is possible, however, that a swell is developing
on which ride people who see inflation as an avoidable curse and
neither the natural state of our economy nor something which can
be turned to the advantage of their organizations. Their expectations may include inflation in low single figures — and it is an
expectation in which they rejoice even if it means lower monetary
incomes for them.

But all the first three groups, if I am right in my estimation of
their expectations (both hopes and fears), expect inflation to
continue, at a lower rate no doubt than in 1979 but at, say, 8 or
9 per cent, which would have seemed dangerous in the 1950s or
1960s. The advent of the SDP in government would probably raise
expectations of higher pay, so that it would be faced with the

prospect of rising prices and a deteriorating pound. Further, if it were suspected that a wages policy was to be imposed, then there would be some jostling for pay increases before the door closed. Given the bureaucratic outlook which pervades the country and the over-manning which those with economic power maintain, there is a very real danger that the sort of monetary package advocated by Mr Jenkins would be swallowed up by higher prices, as the monetarists fear. Further, a different level of expectation may be aroused by technical changes, particularly in communications. New appetites may be stimulated, new hopes kindled.

As long as our present attitudes continue, therefore, there will be pressure for more government spending and inflation. In dealing with these the Alliance should be rather clearer than it now appears to be about whether or not it is in favour of a society thrusting in material terms. I do not call it an expanding society with high growth rates as opposed to a society static in materialist terms because surely everyone is in favour of growth in some directions. One of our difficulties is that the statistics of growth lump everything together — alcohol, tobacco, hideous buildings, uninhabitable blocks of flats. All are regarded as growth. Whether growth is good or bad depends upon your judgement as to the value of the things which are growing. But there is another judgement to be made, a judgement between attitudes and habits of life. For both of these there is something to be said. On the one hand, there are those who argue that a country that is good to live in requires to be a changing, enterprising country in which people work hard, technology is always advancing and the characteristics of a 'race' towards some goal are always present. The exponents of this view will maintain that these features should carry with them a high level of social service, education, care for health and so on, and they will also maintain that only an innovative, industrious country can afford such services. Their opponents argue that the alleged idleness of the British is a positive advantage. No doubt these will say: 'We must use our natural resources better, but we have about enough. We shall be more and more envied by the rat-race countries. Leisure will be of increasing importance. Technology will allow us to work much less.'

Where does the Alliance stand? It has, in the current Parliament, tended to resist the changes that have been put forward as moves in the direction of the 'race'. Is this because, while it is in favour of a more competitive, thrusting economy, it believes these particular proposals (privatization, for example) to be misconceived? Or does it agree with those who see the 'race' as abrasive, reactionary and uncivilized?

At present, unfortunately, Britain seems to be having the worst of both possible worlds. Stimulated by the fear of being left behind and the inflationary nature of our society, every organization is asking for 'more'. So our demands, as evinced by our institutions and authorities, would lead an observer to believe that we favoured a 'racing' society. But the actual conduct of those in charge of our institutions has often seemed to indicate that they favour a static society. If the relative decline of the British economy were the result of a decision to opt for a quieter life with more leisure, there would be much to say for it. But, regrettably, the decline is not the product of any such decision. It is not making for tranquillity but is accompanied by demands for more money, work, gadgets and prestige.

My inclination is to favour the 'race' largely because I believe that there is much poverty to be relieved in Britain and certainly much in, say, Palermo, to which as members of the EEC we cannot be oblivious. Further, if Africa and Asia are to be enriched, this will require trade and investment. Western Europe, with no extra resources with which to buy the goods of the poorer countries or to invest in their development, will not be much help.

But if we are to aim at an expanding economy, then we must make a value judgement about where expansion should come. We must also try to change the expectations of most people: all-round expansion cannot take place everywhere. We shall have to use the state to ensure not only adequate incomes for the poor but also the protection of those who are prepared to accept more leisure instead of more money — for even in expanding society they will be a creditable element. It seems probable that the hours of regular work will be reduced by technology. The voluntary semi-employed, as long as their demands are not excessive, will perform a public service. Expectations will have to be altered, more emphasis put on choice. Do we want to work harder for greater reward or less hard for less reward? The state cannot provide the best of both worlds, more pay for less production.

Further, traditional differentials will have to be modified or abolished. Those who do menial and unpleasant work, at inconvenient hours, in unpleasant circumstances, will have to be paid more; those who do interesting work, in pleasant circumstances, less. I believe that responsibility is actually welcomed by many people. It does not always need extra reward. Certainly, professional work, work which permits the worker to some extent to choose what he does (university research, for instance) and routine administration may have to command fewer rewards.

I do not want to go over again the argument for or against free enterprise and state socialism, but I must reiterate what I take to be the salient points. At the back of the case for socialism in the wide sense lie four arguments. One is the unfairness which still persists among us. This argument, though it certainly points to a change in the way that we run our affairs, is not an argument for nationalization through the creation of public monopolies. The poor do not necessarily gain from this. Indeed, nationalization of the kind recently enacted has harmed them as consumers — the poor are chiefly interested in being able to buy cheaply. Another argument is based on the belief that as free capitalism is collapsing, we must turn to state capitalism. There is no evidence of this. The economy of communist countries is in a far worse shape than that of the free world. Third, nationalization of industry on the British model was supposed to release new motives, as I noted in chapter 1. But state socialism has not succeeded in achieving this laudable aim. Nationalization has not made it easier for the Government, on behalf of.the people, to control and direct the economy. Our industrial troubles, strikes, restrictive practices and so on have been most evident in the nationalized industries. Finally, the 'commanding heights' of industry — the railways, steel, coal, motor car manufacture — have proved far from commanding. On the contrary, they have given Governments of both parties their worst headaches. It is the size and the demands of the nationalized industries which have made the economy so difficult to manage.

The failure of state socialism does not mean that all the ideals and methods of socialism must be abandoned. It does not mean that our society provides enough equality of opportunity or, indeed, enjoyment. It does not mean that we all, as workers and consumers, must give up hope of having more say in the way things are run. It does not mean that the state has no role to play — it has an important role, but is neither the collection of a larger and larger bag of miscellaneous monopolies in public ownership, nor the attempt to plan the use of all means of production, distribution and exchange as well as owning them.

Over most of the economic field consumers can best express their wishes through the market. To ensure that the market works properly in their interest they must have information and they must be protected from monopolies. The Consumers' Association has been very successful at providing information. I cannot say the same for the various government-sponsored efforts in the areas of monopolies and restrictive practices, such as the Monopolies Commission and the Office of Fair Trading. I do not blame such bodies. They suffer, however, from four disabilities. They have little direct touch with consumers, and, unlike the Consumers' Association, have no direct incentive to give consumer satisfaction. They have to work against the grain of much legislation and many habits of mind which encourage monopolies and restrictions. Matters requiring their investigation are apt to reach them late in the day because some crisis has grown up. The criteria by which they are to decide whether mergers may take place is cloudy. For instance, in the case involving the Royal Bank of Scotland, what weight was to be attached to the interests of management, clients, Scottish economic patriotism or the working of the Bank of England's central apparatus? As technology improves communications, the spread of information should be easier. It should also be easier to give warning of monopolistic exploitation at an earlier stage. The public should be enabled to feed back its complaints as information reaches it.

What seems to me crucial to the success of the Alliance is that it should promote a new form of industrial structure with the aim of reforming industrial efficiency and giving those in industry and commerce greater satisfaction from their work and a greater interest in it. I have frequently said that we must get out of our minds that there are only two ways of running any industry of any size, both bureaucratic — either as a bureaucratic nationalized industry or as a bureaucratic private corporation. Although there is much talk in Parliament about encouraging small businesses and even workers' co-operation, yet at the back of the minds of most Ministers and nearly all senior civil servants seems to be the idea that even those forms of business must conform to the structure of the big joint-stock limited company. Anything outside the conventional bonds of the limited company or the state national-ized industry is considered an eccentricity, likely to succeed only on a very small scale.

Many of us who are members of the Alliance came into politics because we were shocked by poverty in the face of affluence; felt that a much better degree of equality should be possible; rejected the notion of men as 'hands' or implements of any sort; while respecting the market economy as a means to freedom and pros-perity, saw it as servant rather than master and wished that its benefits could be more widely spread. The state socialist sees the solution in state ownership. The Liberal Social Democrat sees the solution, or at least I see it myself, in a strong, guiding state enforcing the law, standing for the common good and a decent minimum for all but leaving the management of industry, as far as possible, to those who work in it. 'Industrial relations' should not exist. It should be in the interest of all in industry to work together. This may be an ideal, but our present system presupposes the opposite, which is an absurdity. The organization of industry may take many forms, but the least realistic is that which places workers in opposition to owners and managers.

As in other areas of policy, we must not start with our eyes fixed on Whitehall, nor with too conservative an acceptance of the present methods. I am all for variety in commercial organiza-tions, and no doubt there is a place — rather a small one, I suspect — for the huge monolithic corporation, but neither the state monopolies nor the huge conglomerates have proved very satis-factory (as some of us pointed out long ago). The growth of the regulations jungle and the forms of taxation preferred in this country have favoured big business, which can afford its own staffs of accountants and lawyers. We must improve competition, give the population more of a direct interest in business and cope with the changes which technology will make possible.

Some people ask why, if competition is good for industry, competition between capital and labour should be bad within a capitalist society. Indeed, they maintain that there is an inevitable conflict of interest between capital and labour.

Competition does not give freedom of choice only: it is not only a matter of undercutting and perhaps bankrupting your competitor. It encourages emulation, as does a race. Sir Ronald Walker, who manufactured blankets, used to say that he could tell how good the quality of his blankets was only by comparing them with those of his competitors. It is true that a company has to decide how much of its profit it is going to invest in capital replacement or extension and how much it is going to distribute — and to that extent there is 'competition' between capital and current distribution. But this is a very different type of competition. Various activities might occupy me; to that extent there is competition for my time. But the decision about which to pursue is taken by one entity, myself. So in industry 'competition' between capital and labour is serious only when they have different interests and are in different hands. It must be right, especially after looking at our experiences of the last few years, to try to ensure that capital and labour have, at least in a great measure, the same interests. This is certainly not achieved by state socialism. Here the state, not the worker in the industry, owns the capital, takes the profit or surplus value, if any. I have always wanted to extend the idea that workers should look on managers as working for them.

One obvious way to achieve this is through producers' co-operatives. The objections to these are threefold. It is argued, first, that the workers will not have the long-term interests of the co-operative at heart. They will demand too high a distribution of profits; they will not spend enough on good management or sales promotion; if the co-operative is doing well, they will sell it. This objection arises largely from the unfamiliarity of the co-operative idea. Nor has the danger that it anticipates by any means always materialized in the co-operative world. Second, it is said that co-operatives will be unenterprising, that they will cling to old techniques. An economy dominated by co-operatives would, it is alleged, be resistant to change. (Consumers' co-operatives have tended to be conservative, though this is changing.) The third argument is that many people do not want ownership of, or responsibility for, the business in which they work. It may indeed be prudent to spread one's savings. There is a great concourse of people, many of them excellent workers, many highly skilled, who want to get on with the job, do their work, draw their pay and go home. They do not want to attend management meetings. They are content to leave management to someone else. We have seen how disastrous can be an over-extended notion of democracy. In the Labour Party it has led to some associations falling into the hands of people who have simply out-sat their opponents.

Nevertheless, the principle behind co-ops must surely be valuable. They give some extra satisfaction. At least those with menial and boring jobs feel that they are being treated as partners and can take some interest in the overall direction of the enterprise; they are ends, not merely means. Co-operatives set common goals for workers of all grades, and they ensure that the work force is informed about what is going on. Even workers who have no ambition to own or manage usually like to feel that their views will count if expressed, even if for years on end they have been content to work on contract and to leave discussion to others.

The example of a group of 'pure' co-ops which has lately attracted much notice is that at Mondragon in Spain. By a 'pure' co-operative I mean an undertaking (a) which is owned entirely and directly by the workers, with no outside shareholders, though there may be creditors; (b) in which all, or at least 90 per cent, of the workers are members of the co-operative, so that there is very little, if any, labour on contract; (c) in which the workers own and arrange for the management of the business directly (appointing and dismissing the managers and sharing individually in the ownership, the profits or losses), not simply through a trust acting on their behalf or through the ownership of the shares by their trade union; (d) in which the principle of one man (or woman)/one vote applies — even in those co-ops in which the managers are paid high salaries or the number of shares held by members may vary, such managers or members have only one vote at general meetings. A further feature of Mondragon — which is not essential to a 'pure' co-op — is that salaries and wages must fall within a given range; that is, the top manager may not be paid more than, say, four times the salary of the lowest paid.

But there is infinite variety of 'impurities' which can, to my mind, be introduced into co-operatives without destroying the principle that the workers should have a stake in the business over and above their wages and some say in its destiny. For instance, some shares may be held on behalf of the workers by a trust, thus lessening the danger that the members may look too much to their individual short-term advantage. Some experts may be employed on contract without being members; even some wholly distinct outside shareholding may be allowed. If, however, there is too much dilution, then the sense of common ownership is destroyed. If all or a substantial proportion of employees get their livelihood very largely from their wages and not from the share in the enterprise to which their membership entitles them, their motives will not differ substantially from those working in non co-operative employment.

Not everyone is agreed on the reasons for the success of the Mondragon co-operatives — nor, indeed, on whether they will continue to be successful. To my mind, however, they are a most valuable experiment, in which the following features should especially be noticed.

They were a local initiative started by Father Arismende, not only without aid from the central government but even in some defiance of it. They harnessed Basque patriotism to self-help. It has long seemed to me that they set an example which local British patriotism might follow. There was, and still is, an up-surge of patriotic feeling in Scotland, but so conservative are the British, and so nurtured on the twin beliefs that little or nothing can be done without government assistance and that assistance must come from London, that this patriotism, diverted into conventional political channels — as it has turned out, ineffectively — has not moved the Scots to improve their own economy without the aid of central government. Both in Scotland and the regions of England and in Wales and Northern Ireland local disgust at the rate of unemployment and local patriotism should be channelled into action on the lines propounded by Father Arismende.

Mondragon is the centre of a group of seventy or more co-operatives (the number increases annually). This solves many problems. There is diversity of employment. If one co-operative hits a bad patch in the market, the others will help it. Co-operatives are at their best — perhaps, in their 'pure' form, possible at all — only if the membership of each is not too large (Mondragon is inclined to think that 800 employees is about the maximum). But a group of co-operatives can support services such as technical training and financial advice on a scale that would be beyond the means of one small business. And the co-operatives are linked with the communities which support them, supplying in turn training schemes and welfare services.

At the heart of the operation is the Bank Caja Laboral Popular. This not only takes local deposits, which it lends to the co-operatives, but also vets all proposals for new co-operatives and supervises the management of the whole group. It has been objected that the bank exercises too much control but, as far as I am aware, it has not undermined the feeling of partnership with which Mondragon is imbued. It is itself, of course, a co-operative.

To import Mondragon methods into this country might be difficult. Conventional thinking in the trade unions, management and government is against them; nor would they suit us in every way. But apart from the improvement in efficiency and industrial relations which would flow from Mondragon-like experiments, they would meet other difficulties which face us.

Lately there has been a growing interest in co-operatives around Britain. This has been fostered by various agencies — for instance, the Co-operative Development Association, Job Ownership Limited and Icom. Most of the new co-operatives are very small, embracing at most 200 or 300 members. Several have run into initial difficulties, which is not to be wondered at, given the state of the British economy, the resistance of certain vested interests and the unfamiliarity of the principles and practice of workers' co-operation.

The field which has hardly been tapped and which, it seems to me, should be tackled is that occupied by the public industries and services. It is in the public sector that I see most progress being made towards co-operation. In Italy track maintenance and station repairs on the nationalized railways are put out to tender; at least one co-operative has won a large contract. Refuse collection, the running of restaurant services (already there is one buffet run by those who work in it), possibly services on the motorways and parts of the nationalized industries could be hived off to co-operatives. In the course of time I see the co-operative principle being applied to the industries themselves. It is not necessary to 'privatize' national industries by the conventional means of returning them to big business. They lie under the hand of government, which could turn part of them over to the workers. The move towards management buy-outs should also be encouraged.

In the private sector I should like to see help for co-operatives being offered by new banking facilities. I hope that the public authorities would encourage nests of co-operatives in different parts of the country. These authorities are large employers of labour and avid consumers of goods. They are already beginning to hive off some of their activities (refuse collection, for example). If local transport, refuse collection, road maintenance and perhaps house repairs were handed over to co-ops, we should be able to build up groups more self-reliant and more likely to be successful than isolated co-operatives could hope to be. Some government agencies themselves might be turned into co-operatives.

I should also like to see large companies, especially conglomerates, broken up into cells, some controlled by the workers. Mr Norman Macrae has written most persuasively on this topic;* I trust that the Alliance will pick up his ideas. Co-operatives are not the only way by which co-operation can be spread. They are a means to an end — an end which can be approached from other directions. I am under no illusions about the possibility or desirability of running industry through a series of workers' soviets. The basis of ideas such as those of Norman Macrae, as I understand it, is that modern psychology and technology have rendered unnecessary (except in a few cases) the great concentrations of labour that one sees at Detroit or Coventry, for example. Modern technology can allow for dispersal with adequate means of instant communication. The group that is given a target but is free to decide how that is to be achieved is in tune with modern beliefs.

* See, for example, 'The Coming Entrepreneurial Revolution', *Economist*, 25 December 1976.

Men and women will increasingly prefer to work for different spells, at different times and, indeed, in different places. They will be able to arrange their own timetables, work in smaller groups and still contribute to large enterprises.

The armed services show us how large units can be articulated as smaller cells, answering to a common purpose but to some extent regulating themselves. The platoon commander and the sergeant draw up their own schemes for implementing the wider plan of the batallion; the batallion commander does the same in relation to his brigade; and so on. The flow of information in British industry seems greatly inferior to that of the Army, the Navy or the Air Force. British management often seems further removed from the shop floor than is the colonel from his men, despite the hierarchical structure of the Army. Nor does there seem to be the chance of promotion within British industry which exists in other countries. In fact, the very idea of 'working up', common in the USA, seems rare in Britain.

We might learn too from Japan. The Japanese appear to operate an efficient and thrusting economy without sacrificing unity in the firm. Certain aspects of the Japanese system seem repugnant to Liberals: its indenturing of young men and women at an early age for the rest of their lives, the web of company relationships in which they seem to be involved, a certain ruthlessness. But if I understand the Japanese system aright, it has certain advantages. It seems to generate solidarity and loyalty among the workers in a company. The Japanese are apparently educated to rate work in business more highly than we do. While Japanese company structure is founded on a discipline which we may lack, I am told that there is more mingling of different grades outside work, when criticisms of management are made freely to managers. The big companies seem to be better articulated both internally and with their external satellites.

I am told — and I emphasize that I have no direct experience — that Japanese workers accept that their work is more than the earning of a wage or salary. They acknowledge not only their own obligations to their fellow workers but also their companies' obligations to the community. I am informed that one department staffed by girls was offered a bonus for increasing output. After a few days they asked that their bonus be cancelled because it was unfair, indeed dishonest; their increase depended almost entirely on work done in other departments. I also learn that in some companies employees are expected to choose wives or husbands from within the company.

I do not see how an Alliance Government could impose Japanese attitudes — I do not admire all those attitudes, nor would I like to see them imposed even if that were possible. But I believe it would be a step forward if some of the causes of our troubles were recognized and Japanese methods studied. We are told that British industry is 'non-competitive' and that the cure for that is to submit it to ruthless competition. But in addition to competition British industry requires, to my mind, stronger ties within firms, a greater appreciation of the common interests of management and labour and a common understanding of the needs of the country.

If a move in the direction indicated were possible, would a permanent incomes policy be necessary? I would hope not, because as more workers become directly interested in the fortunes of their companies they will be less inclined to demand insupportable wage increases. But there would need to be a change in the nationalized industries. I have said that I believe some shift is essential for the running of the economy. More must be put into the market. The breaking up of some of the monopolies in the public sector is as important as the reduction of its overall size. As with all the reforms which I hope the Alliance will embrace, the object should be to spread power and responsibility, to marry enterprise to communal benefit and to increase choice. If at present the demand seems to be for more decisions to be taken by officials, this is, I believe, because officials or their representatives are the most vocal. As their standard of living and education rises, people will demand a bigger say in determining the use of their money and the balance between work and leisure. This the Alliance should welcome.

In this process the entrepreneur will be of crucial importance. If British industry has suffered from a lack of common purpose in business and from too little commitment to the community, it has also suffered from the neglect of the mainspring of a free economy, the individual innovator. There is an immense literature on management and on the trade unions. We discuss the education needed for those who work in industry, the size and distribution of factories, the ownership of firms and so on. For years criticism has been levied at the amateur nature of much industrial leadership and, even more, at the failure of our political leaders and civil servants to understand the technocrat. It has been suggested that part of our economic failure is due to the unsuccessful attempts of an outdated social and political system trying to cope with a technocratic age. These are important matters but I would say that the failure to grant the entrepreneur his due is even more serious. We fail to distinguish him from the manager who takes on an existing and defined job. Ever since I have been in the House of Commons I have listened to and made speeches in praise of small businesses. But the small business which is, say, an established shop is very different from the small business newly created by an entrepreneur.

There is a school of thought which believes that the day of the entrepreneur is over. Invention, so the argument runs, is now the result of team research. Success in business requires the services of experts of many kinds. There is some truth in this assertion. But the great majority of innovations are developed by small companies. What makes the employment of large teams necessary is, to a great extent, the myriad regulations handed down by Governments and the firm grip of accountants, financiers and lawyers. There is room for doubt about the necessity for, and the usefulness of, such controls. In any case, I believe that the entrepreneur has a vital part to play.

What is an entrepreneur? Essentially someone who likes business, who particularly likes running his or her own business and who enjoys taking risks. Entrepreneurs are usually addicted to a gamble: they are often difficult members of any team, but it is quite unjust to assume that they are selfish, ambitious buccaneers, almost spivs. Unfortunately for them, they usually do not fit into tidy, bureaucratic patterns. In my experience they are comparatively rare birds. If our educational and social system is antipathetic to industry and trade in general, it is even more disdainful of the entrepreneur, so that entrepreneurial talent often withers before it has had much of a chance to show itself. I reckon that in the time that I have known Orkney and Shetland, say forty years, the 37,000 or so inhabitants of those islands have produced three or four full-blooded entrepreneurs and perhaps five times as many men and women with entrepreneurial instincts. I leave out of this calculation the highly enterprising fishing community which lives in a world of its own. Whether that is typical of Britain as a whole I do not know. Entrepreneurs are important not only for the wealth they produce and the employment they provide but also because they are the innovators, the yeast in the economy. And all the entrepreneurs I have known, though lone birds in many cases, have been interested in their communities and partly at least moved by public spirit. Socialism — I do not mean state socialism only but the whole gamut of socialist ideas, the socialist reaction against poverty, oppression, exploitation — has never devised a place for the entrepreneur, and that is a great failing which the Alliance should seek to correct. If the type of socialism without the state which I favour, and which Mondragon in some respects exemplifies, is to succeed, it must find a place for the entrepreneur — the genuine entrepreneur, not the financial gambler who will usually find a place for himself. Nor, valuable as they may be, do I refer to the managers of established businesses. The parable of the talents is rather neglected on the Liberal left. The point of that parable is that it is a sin, not a virtue, to play safe.

Such changes in industrial structure must bear upon the trade unions. If they are to find a new role consonant with the needs and aspirations of modern industrial workers, they must play their part in taking more responsibility for the efficient running of industry. Unless their members are convinced that trade unions advance their interests, the unions will wither away. But their insistence on wage rates which cannot be justified by performance, on the maintenance of restrictive practices, on over-manning and resistance to industrial change is at present often harmful to the interests of their members. Nor do they represent the poorest in the nation. They could have an important part to play in encouraging co-operation, as some union leaders are doing. By dropping their advocacy of the closed shop and seeking membership only among those who see the advantage of membership, they would open the door to a new lease on useful life. They could use their funds for productive investment on behalf of their members. They should also be willing to enter into binding contracts as to wages, conditions of employment and so on, for breaches of which they would be liable to pay damages out of their funds. Already some contracts lasting for two or three years have been negotiated, with advantages to both employers and workers.

I have mentioned investment and the difficulty and importance of ensuring that investment is made in the right areas. The British financial system is very centralized. We are reduced to four major clearing banks. In Scotland there are three joint-stock banks where there used to be eight, and one is a wholly owned subsidiary of an English bank. Most small savers consider the only outlets for their money to be building societies or Government securities, often bought through the savings bank. Local savings are thus drained off from the areas where they accumulate, and a large proportion is invested unproductively.

The Alliance, I hope, will reform the investment channels. Either the savings banks should be turned into conduits through which local savings will be able to reach local industry, or new channels must be cut. This will be a departure from current practice, but it is a departure the first steps of which can already be seen. Small merchant banks have now established themselves in Scotland. Noble Grossart in Edinburgh was one of the first of these and the original partners, Iain Noble and Michael Grossart, should be consulted. Mr Noble has already given considerable attention to local finance apart from development of his estate in Skye. I have suggested that the ICFC and the Highlands and Islands Development Board are suitable existing instruments for investment. Might they not accept local deposits as well as making local loans? And might they or the savings banks or perhaps the Co-operative Bank perform some of the advisory and supervisory tasks of the Caja Laboral Popular? To suggest that this is not to ignore the work of the existing joint-stock banks, but unless they alter their ways they will remain centralized institutions, not particularly orientated to local risk investment. Some of the smaller merchant banks might, however, meet the bill.

John Plender, in his enlightening book *That s the Way the Money Goes*, has shown that the investment of money is more and more carried out by big institutions. According to him, at the time he was writing (1981) they were buying shares from individual investors to the value of £20 million a week. The fifteen biggest investors in stocks and shares, all insurance companies and pension funds, each controlled investments in excess of £1 billion; in the case of the largest, the Prudential, their value was in excess of £7 billion. Thus the investment of savings is highly centralized. It is predominantly in huge companies and property.

Mr Plender goes on to examine the policies of these giants and their success. Traditionally they have not interfered with the running of the companies in which they hold shares. They have simply tried to fund profitable investment in the interests of themselves and their shareholders. He points out that the institutions have not been conspicuously successful. They were deeply involved in the property boom of 1972—3, which largely collapsed. Chapter 5 of his book, which gives an account of the extensive network of interests that links the pension funds, the merchant banks and the property speculators, should be studied with care and alarm by the Alliance.

Mr Plender also draws attention to the way in which private and public share dealings are sometimes confused. But, from the point of view of the economy, perhaps the most serious lesson to be drawn from his book is that funds of this size must inevitably channel savings into large established markets. With such huge portfolios, investors are bound to look to large companies, or office blocks, or the more expensive pictures and other art objects. They now have very big overseas investments. As a result, they cannot show any striking successes. Their portfolios resemble each other. The worker in private industry, after paying contributions throughout his working life, finds that his pension has seldom kept pace with inflation. It then has to be topped up out of current profits, to the detriment of current workers and investors. Mr Plender ends by asking: 'To what end have the British people handed over £100 billion of their money to this powerful new financial estate?' The answer is that certainly the City has benefited. But the benefits for British industry, especially new and small industries, are less apparent.

There is little or no case, in my view, for pension funds in the public sector, where pensions are guaranteed ultimately by the taxpayer; better that contributions should be made straight to the Exchequer. In the private sector investment should be decentralized and greater freedom of choice left to the investor. Conservatives and believers in the free market usually urge all sorts of objections to forced savings. But forced savings are now a major feature of our economy. It is not at all clear that in times of inflation such savings are a good bet; neither is it clear that the institutions have proved much less wasteful than Governments in investing their new levies. And, of course, they open up an easy route for state control. Why bother with a shopping list of companies to be nationalized when all a socialist Government needs to do is to take over the major pension funds? To my mind, the structure and operations of the City should in the long term engage the attention of the Alliance just as much as the structure of government.

As outlined above, its operations should be decentralized. As far as the management of currency and credit are concerned, I am unfitted to provide a solution, but the problem has engaged economists for a long time and is surely not insoluble. In theory, the Government as owner of the Bank of England, controls currency and credit. But the principles on which they are created remain obscure. Money is in one sense a commodity, but it is a commodity created by fiat. The Government pays for borrowing its own commodity, and the national debt has reached large proportions (mitigated by inflation). Though the operations of industry seem to have little effect on the creation of credit, its availability greatly affects industry. There must surely be something wrong when dealing in currencies is more profitable than making goods.

The Alliance should build on what is already happening in connection with the recruiting of local savings for local initiative. There is no reason why the pattern should be uniform. In the north of Scotland the Highlands and Islands Development Board is to hand; in the rest of Scotland, and indeed overlapping the Board, some merchant bankers are interested in this type of development. Further south there are the Co-operative Bank and some regional finance houses (for example, Dartington in Bristol). This country is too conditioned by centralization to be able to follow the example of Mondragon at once. An Alliance Government should offer support to local banks or trusts by guaranteeing at least a minimum interest on deposits placed with them. Though I envisage local businesses paying fees for advice and services supplied, the Government might bear part of the cost of setting up the legal, accountancy and management units required.

To sum up these proposals for industrial policy: they are intended to allow workers to take a more direct interest in the companies in which they work. I recognize that the degree to which workers want to play an active part in running a company varies from worker to worker and from year to year. But I believe that the great majority of workers wish to be informed about their company's affairs, and most at any rate want to be consulted about its objectives and management. For some, more active participation in day-to-day management would compensate for the drawbacks of routine work, particularly if extra effort and the success of the company led directly to their sharing in the profits. As a step towards this objective, it would seem useful to encourage smaller units of production. In many cases such units should be co-operatives of some kind, 'pure' or 'impure'. These units might be linked regionally around a mother bank such as the Caja Laboral Popular, or they might be part of a larger organization, as suggested by Mr Norman Macrae and as I believe is the case in Japan. From the point of view of the country as a whole such a system, operating within the market, would give a better service to the consumer. It would decrease industrial friction, promote greater concern for the success of industry and commerce and spread rewards more widely. It would do something to repair one of the fissures — that between capital and labour, managers and men — which distort our society, and it would enhance the standing of the employed, a large majority of the nation.

Governing Britain

6

Social Services: Co-operation and Community

A gulf extends between those who would like to see the welfare services expanded until they embrace every aspect of life and those who hope that as we all become richer they can be contracted. I belong to the latter school. I willingly accept that there will always be unfortunate members of the community who, because of their disabilities, have to be helped. But I would like to see us moving towards an ideal state of affairs in which everyone who is physically and mentally normal can run his or her own life and make his or her own decisions. This would entail not only generating more wealth but also ensuring that the poor get very much richer. The ideal may be a long way off. For years to come there will be people who, though perfectly healthy, require help. Our aim should be not to increase but to decrease their numbers. Ideally, I would like to see everyone have enough money to buy not only adequate food, housing, heating and so on but also education and medical attention.

The other school of thought does not only merely dispute the possibility of the withering away of the state-run welfare services; it denies that such a withering is desirable. It would like to see more and more provision by the state, more and more decisions made for us by councils and bureaucrats. It holds that individual freedom to choose destroys equality and sets up the stresses of envy and competition. It would maintain that a country in which everyone had to use state-provided services and education would be more cohesive. It would argue that civil servants make better decisions than do individuals. It fears that individual choice introduces the vice of the market place, greed, into areas of human conduct in which it is inappropriate.

This is in some respects a barren dispute, since those who want to extend state provision — at least those outside the extreme left of the Labour Party and the communists — do not believe that in practice the services of the state can be extended except slowly, and those who look forward to the retraction of the state do not believe that it can happen all at once. But I think that the debate reflects an important distinction between conflicting aims which should be constantly borne in mind when we frame current policies. If we are asked to set up new services or extend existing ones, we should ask why, in a rich society, these should be necessary. As the existing services should be helping to put themselves out of business, are the new measures necessitated by some fault in their working? Or have we genuinely uncovered new sources of social evil which require new services to eradicate them? Since the war the social services have grown until they absorb over 23 per cent of GDP and a huge body of educated manpower. This, like other parts of the bureaucracy, has become an interest on its own. It has developed its own momentum, which is fuelled from within the service and not by outside demand. It has an interest in retaining clients and dependants, not in helping them to stand on their own feet.

There are many socialists, and probably many SDP members and Liberals, who for doctrinaire or pragmatic reasons would be happy to see the state-run welfare services extended. Though she has herself willingly bowed to the opinion of the majority, Mrs Shirley Williams is by no means the only member of the Alliance who would like to see state education extended at the expense of the private schools. As far as I know, only Stephen Haseler, Douglas Eden and those who agree with them have shown any interest in the various proposals for extending individual choice in the services. Some of those in the Alliance who would not advocate any extension of the welfare services usually resist all cuts and are not sympathetic to new methods of running the services. Liberal councillors, for instance, though they have sometimes done a good job in restraining extravagance, have shown little surprise or alarm at the growth of the local authority welfare services. Yet if education were effective, it would be turning out adults better able to run their own lives; if preventive medicine were effective there would be less need for curative medicine.

Dependence upon charity — whether private or state — and surrender of decision-making to others, however well qualified, is debilitating. The old and inspiring statement 'The poorest he that is in England has a life to live as the richest he' to me means that all of us should have not only adequate sustenance but also freedom to make our own decisions, indeed to live our own lives. Respect seems to me to be at the root of a decent community, and that means that neither the state nor anyone else should take over the running of people's lives. If they are adult, healthy and sane, we must respect their right to carve out their own future, as long as they do not harm or constrict others. To make choice possible by providing opportunities and some basic wealth is to show respect for the individual; to force people to accept what is handed to them is to show disrespect, and the same reasoning which led to the abolition of truck should militate against it.

To hold this view is not to put the case for extreme individualism. At present, as I have remarked, what is fragmenting the country is not extreme individualism but the demands of organizations. I argued in *The Common Welfare*, and still maintain, that we have neglected the community — or, rather, its positive side, its responsibilities as opposed to its rights. But while I would still look to the community and the family as the matrix of true welfare, I am now impressed both by the need to regenerate some more national concept of the common welfare, perhaps embracing Western Europe, and by the need, mentioned in *The Common Welfare*, to involve us all, and particularly the recipients in the organization of welfare services.

Having given some indication of what I regard as the purpose of the welfare services, it is time briefly to describe what they are. Within the term 'welfare service' I include health, public housing, assistance with travel costs and transport subsidies (in so far as they are designed to help individuals) and the more strictly defined social services provided by the public social welfare departments. At this stage I also include welfare payments, unemployment, sickness pay and so on. I realize that this is to extend the phrase 'welfare service' to cover a very broad range of amenities. It will be necessary in time to break it down. Here I lump together all those services in kind and transfer payments by which the state attempts to assist individuals to a higher standard of life or to make good the handicaps under which they or the districts in which they live may labour.

It is calculated that by the end of the century the welfare services, together with education, defence expenditure and the other costs of government will account for half of Britain's GDP. This means that over three-quarters of the effort of the workers will be taken and spent by the government. The purposes for which this expenditure may be used at present and the methods of its administration are largely determined centrally, though the actual disbursement or service may be local. Although some assistance (for example, over travel) is available only in certain parts of Britain, most of the services or payments are provided according to criteria which are national. Another feature of the social services is their incredible and growing complexity. Just as no one can understand the tax system, few people are aware of their entitlement to various benefits. Logic has long since departed. This complexity is to some extent both the effect and the cause of the enormous rise in the number of officials required to administer the services. It leads to injustice, waste, dissatisfaction and a huge output of literature attempting to explain and deal with ever-growing mountains of regulations.

In the short run, once again, the Alliance will have to work within the limits of comprehension evinced by the electorate and the existing organization. But it must move towards a fairer and simpler system, one which will direct us down the road that I have indicated and will be less wasteful of resources. The proposals, largely drafted by Mr Dick Taverne, which the SDP agreed at its 1982 Conference, seem right to me. They include a basic benefit with three main components, a child credit, a housing credit and a personal credit. The working poor will receive higher benefits, which will help to eliminate the poverty trap. The extra allowance which married men receive will be abolished in recognition of the fact that in many families today husband and wife both work and that it is the single parent who is usually worst off. The proposed benefits would be selective — that is to say, aimed at the poor — and not universal, as are many of the present payments and concessions. I believe them to represent a big step in the right direction, making social security fairer (for instance, no longer could a rise in wages make a worker worse off) and simpler. But I believe that we must go further still.

The next move must be in the direction of a national minimum income available to all whose incomes fall below the minimum, irrespective of whether their misfortunes arise from sickness, accident, unemployment, ill-luck or old age. If someone is threatened with penury, it does not matter whether the cause is industrial accident, sickness or inability to work. He or she must be helped. A minimum income or reverse income tax will ensure that everyone's means are automatically brought up to a minimum standard. Further, those in employment who are paid at a rate below what is considered minimal should have their wages increased by the state. There may have to be modifications, some provision for special cases. (Schemes were originally worked out by Lady Rhys-Williams, and the notion of a reverse income tax has been further developed by her son, Sir Brandon Rhys-Williams.) Such a move would be a sensible advance on Beveridge.

Two preliminary points must be made. A difficulty is raised by people who deliberately, or through gross incompetence, reduce their incomes below the minimum. Small farmers give away their farms and live on national assistance; sometime millionaires plead poverty; old ladies who have saved for their last years find that they are expected to contribute to the cost of the homes to which they are eventually forced to go while their less thrifty sisters live in them free. The difficulty to my mind is genuine, but it already exists. I incline to think that there is no wholly satisfactory way around it. At least as the welfare services move towards cash payments or vouchers for all, the large sums which are apparently spent now on special cases (for example, on invalids who are flown home from San Francisco at £21,000) will be put to different uses. The second point is that there will have to be certain extra payments, though I believe that these need not proliferate. Children, dependants and others should be entitled to their own incomes.

We must get it out of the heads of the electorate that to alter the form of the social services is somehow to hurt the poor, to favour the rich. On the contrary, the very people who have a great deal to gain from the reform of the services are the recipients. By sweeping away the farrago of different rates and conditions and replacing them with a minimum income or reverse income tax, we shall both save resources and help the recipients: the only losers will be some bureaucrats.

Two books written by men of different political opinions show just how twisted the Beveridge schemes have become. In *Charge** Arthur Seldon shows that in 1974 households of two adults and two children with an income of between £1,749 and £2,115 received £658 in social benefits for a contribution of £685 in taxes. To achieve this slightly negative result a regiment of officials is employed. Mr Seldon shows too that under the redistribution provisions in force in 1976, which have not changed much since, the only groups who enjoyed a net gain were single adults and families with four children. He also points out that a high pro-portion of the payments made by way of tax and contribution for welfare services are 'abortive' — that is to say, they return to the taxpayers: 'The 6,051 households paid just over £7 million in taxes and received over £3¼ million in benefits. In all therefore 46 per cent or not far short of half of the taxes were refunded in benefits to the very same households' (p. 160).

This theme, that the present system of attempting to help the needy and to redistribute wealth has resulted in a vast and point-less machinery for collecting and redistributing money to the same people, many of them members of the well-to-do middle classes, has been expanded by Julian Le Grand in *The Strategy of Equality*.† He takes a rather wider conspectus than Arthur Seldon and looks not only at social security, education, health, housing and environ-mental services (he also considers defence) but also at the subsidies paid in the fields of transport, law and order and the personal social services as well as overseas aid.

Le Grand shows that in every sphere of the social services it is the better off, those with middle-range incomes, who receive the

* London: Temple Smith, 1977.
† London: Allen and Unwin, 1982.

lion's share. His main thesis is that we should be promoting greater equality of well-being. This, in his view, cannot be achieved through the social services. As far as health is concerned, the dominant influence is income, and this cannot be offset by education or services in kind. Children of the professional classes are still, after at least twenty-five years of the National Health Service (NHS), four times more likely to survive their first year than are those of manual workers. They are also likely to live five years longer. At every stage in life the professional classes make more use of, and benefit more from, the health services than do the lower-income groups. On education he writes that 'while public expenditure on compulsory education slightly favours the lower social groups, expenditure on the post-compulsory sectors strongly favours the better off.' Members of the working class, as might be expected, emerge with far fewer educational qualifications than do members of the middle classes.

Mr Le Grand's findings on housing, though open to question, are more surprising — indeed, alarming. Large resources have been spent since the war (and were before it) on not only the provision of public housing but also better housing for the poor and a fairer distribution of aid to promote greater choice. The policies pursued have manifestly failed. This is to some extent because of the obstinate folly of architects. The tower blocks and the bleak housing estates which infest our cities have offered housing which even the poor reject as soon as they can. But while it is true that a large proportion of public expenditure on housing has been directed to the poor, if the whole system of rebates, the reduction of tax allowed on mortgages and the number of middle-class families who accept public housing (especially in Scotland) is taken into account, then the balance in favour of the poor is not nearly so pronounced. Indeed, if you ignore rates and hold that owner-occupiers should pay for imputed income, it is clear that the poor are not favoured at all. Mr Le Grand states: 'The fundamental reason why the better off have better living conditions is because they are better off and there is not a great deal that housing policy of whatever kind can do about that' (p. 103). (The latest Budget provisions increasing tax relief on mortgages make the situation worse.)

The same conclusions — that public subsidies out of taxation or the provision of welfare services have failed to achieve equality and, indeed, on balance have been of more use to the middle-income groups than to the lower — are even more pertinent in the case of public transport. Of current grants to assist public transport 44 per cent goes to the British Rail transport services. Mr Le Grand writes: 'The richest fifth of the population spends ten times as much on rail travel as does the poorest fifth' (p. 107). He concludes: 'Public expenditure on the social services has not achieved equality in any of its interpretations.'

I myself demonstrated, I hope, in *The Common Welfare* that twenty-five years after the Beveridge Report* and all the additions made to the social services since its inception, the difference between the prosperous and poorer districts remained almost as marked as ever. Further, in the poorer districts the number of people who were dependent upon the state was increasing. In 1973—4 supplementary benefit was running at 146.6 per cent of the national average in Northern Ireland, 123.1 per cent in Scotland but only 67.5 per cent in East Anglia. In Newcastle-upon-Tyne in 1975—6 13.8 per cent of the population under 18 was in residential care, compared with 5.7 per cent on the Isle of Wight. By the tests of education, health, employment and the likelihood of staying out of prison (or resisting the attentions of criminals) the chances of a child in Bournemouth were far superior to those of his contemporaries in Sunderland.

From these figures I deduced that the present welfare services did too little to raise the standard of the community. And having argued earlier in the book that politics were about values, and that these values pertained to the states of mind and activities of individuals who were greatly dependent upon the community, there could be no question that all individuals would be given a chance to reach their full potential until communities were improved. This could not be achieved by enforcing uniformity but by helping each community to realize its full potential. This in turn entailed the involvement of the community in its own development. Yet the social services were handed down from above. Further, they stepped in only when an individual was poverty-stricken, ill or in other difficulties. They were not, as they should be, preventative.

* *Social Insurance and Allied Services*, Cmnd 6404, London: HMSO, 1942.

The Alliance has come into the field at a time when we should think again about the purposes and methods of the welfare services. I would hope that it would pay close attention to the arguments of Arthur Seldon and Julian Le Grand. Let me restate the main faults of the welfare services.

They are now extremely complicated and highly bureaucratic. They encourage a passive attitude among their clients and engender widespread incomprehension among all classes. As Professor Peter Drucker has pointed out,* there is a growing conflict of interest between the beneficiaries of the services and those who pay for them. Instead of being a unifying force in the community, they are becoming a divisive one, partly because of the division between takers and providers but also because some of the services are so inefficient and unsatisfactory that more and more people contract out. They result in the collection of money and its repayment to the same people. If the process were short-circuited, not only would it be more economical because the middlemen, the collectors and dispersers, could be cut out, but also better use would be made of the money. The services have not led to equality of any sort between either individuals or districts.

What are the reforms that are needed? One is certainly to increase the incomes of the poor. I have mentioned already the need for a national minimum income. Mr Le Grand, in a letter to me, says he has calculated that if all subsidies for health care, education, housing (including tax expenditures) and transport had been eliminated in 1978–9, this would have saved nearly £26 billion. If this sum had been given directly to the poorest 20 per cent of the population, it would have more than quadrupled their incomes in that fiscal year. Not that he or I would recommend anything quite as drastic at one blow, but, as he goes on to point out, even by cutting only some of the subsidies to the comparatively rich, the poorest could have had their incomes increased by 60 per cent. The principle behind my suggestion of a minimum income and that of a reverse income tax is essentially the same. The reverse income tax may, however, be more flexible and, since it has long been discussed, is probably the more familiar. At any rate, it seems highly desirable that the Alliance should

* 'Are Unions Becoming Irrelevant?', *Wall Street Journal*, 22 September 1982.

move with all possible speed towards such a scheme, which should cover all those welfare payments which are now made in cash to individuals.

To my mind, it should also enable subsidies for housing and transport to be eliminated. As far as transport is concerned, the incomes of the poor in such places as London and the outer islands — if it is suggested that they face peculiar difficulties over transport — could be further supplemented or their taxation could be reduced.

I find the question of payment for doctors and hospitals more difficult. Arthur Seldon, in chapter 5 of *Charge*, mounts a telling criticism of the finance of the health service. In his view, it has not done away with the 'rationing' of medical care — it is now rationed by time and, to some extent, by influence. Health care is not a 'public good' (preventative medicine is). The present system has led to the starvation of the service, so that we spend less on medical services than do most countries in Western Europe and much less than does the USA. By invoking more individual choice, we could approximate more nearly the optimum use of resources. If the service is thought to be 'free', one encourages unnecessary use of scarce resources. His preferred solution would be to issue vouchers which entitle the individual to insure against the need for treatment. He or she would be free to 'top up' these vouchers and so obtain a higher rate of insurance. Alternatively, as I understand it, he would change to a mixed system in which the state bears part, perhaps most, of the cost but the patient is called upon to bear either a proportion of the provision or a slice of the doctor's or hospital's costs. With this can be allied cash assistance to the very poor (though with a guaranteed minimum income this might be to a large extent unnecessary). Mr Seldon has expanded his argument in a paper delivered in April 1982.* In this he alleges that the NHS has come more and more under the thumb of politicians and bureaucrats; we have lost thousands of doctors through emigration; our hospitals are falling behind; and patients are increasingly turning to private medicine. He recommends that 'the more wealthy 5 per cent will pay, as in America, Australia, Canada and Europe, out of their pockets. The vast middlemass

* *Wither the Welfare State*, Institute of Economic Affairs Occasional Paper No. 60.

will pay with the aid of insurance, though bearing part of each bill out of their pockets. The lowest-income 10 per cent will pay through insurance. They will buy with the aid of government tax credits, cards, vouchers or other devices.' I am not sure how his last proposal will work. But, leaving that aside, I have reservations about the broad aspects of his proposals.

Is the insurance that he advocates to be compulsory? If so, it seems to me that it may not reduce demands on the health service by very much. People will still want to get something for the proportion of the insurance they pay. It will, of course, also make some inroad in freedom of choice. If it is not to be compulsory, what are we to do with those who have not insured and cannot pay? Are we to say to someone who has been run over in the street or is suffering from cancer that if he is not insured and has no money, he must go without medical attention? I do not believe that we could or should. I sympathize with the spirit behind David Owen's statement, 'The existence of the NHS is a constant challenge to the values of the market place; it persistently asserts that there are other values than those determined by money.'* I have always believed that there are aspects of public policy which should be outside the market place and carried on for criteria other than those of profit. Indeed, I believe that many of our troubles stem from confusion on this topic. State control – for example, through the nationalized industries – has introduced the market place into regions to which it does not belong. Socialism, as we know, has failed to replace materialism with altruism. Mr Seldon does not propose that the best medical care should simply be sold to the richest bidder. As I have shown, he favours a system of publicly assisted insurance and incomes supplement. Mr Le Grand is certainly not a devotee of the crude market, given the present distribution of wealth. As he says: 'The effect on equality of abolishing the NHS would depend crucially upon what was done with the public funds that were saved thereby. If these were used to increase the cash incomes of the poor, then it is likely that greater equality, at least in some senses of the term, would be achieved.'† Until radical improvement in the incomes of the poor

* *Face the Future*, p. 377.
† *The Strategy of Equality*, p. 48.

is achieved he advocates a programme of education and a deliberate slanting of expenditure on health services to the poorer areas
— but he is not optimistic about the impact of such policies.

To me, illness and death are in a class of their own among
human disasters. The one certain achievement for the good of
humanity would be the diminution of deaths in childbirth and
of young children. I should hate to think that parents might be
deterred from seeking proper medical attention because their
insurance had run out or because they were unable to 'top it up'.
Nor do I relish the thought of the anxiety which might be caused
just at moments when invalids and their families were least able to
bear it. For the time being, therefore, I should advise the Alliance
to support the health service, though allowing private medicine to
coexist: indeed, the Alliance should encourage it. Mutual support
of private and public services is growing in some hospitals, to the
advantage of all patients. Just as the public service provides some
resources for private patients against welcome payments, so private
medicine can aid the public service. It may be possible to devise a
general system of insurance which 'tops up' the public service. At
present, choice in this regard is limited. In rural areas and small
towns people must in practice accept the local doctors and take
their advice. But once lower incomes have been raised (and perhaps
even now in some places where they have already been raised)
experiments with insurance and vouchers might be tried. On one
matter there is general agreement: that is, that preventative and
public health services are 'public goods' and must be provided by
public authorities, national or local. After the introduction of a
minimum income the most far-reaching and potentially beneficial
change in the running of the welfare services would be to involve
the community and the recipients of such services in their management.

On the finance of housing I differ to some extent from the
Social Democrats, who see public rented housing, built and maintained by the local authorities, as providing the bulk of accommodation. In his book David Owen writes of the 'damaging shift of
financial resources into house purchase'. The property boom
triggered off by the Conservative Government of 1972 may well
have been harmful. But I do not believe that house building for

private sale is damaging, nor would I have thought that house purchase hurts the economy. At present when a house (as Dr Owen admits) is a good investment — unlike, alas, investment in much of industry — and eagerly sought by those who have raised their income, and when the builders are short of orders, I would have thought it unwise of the Alliance to appear to be against home ownership. The addiction of the Scots to cheap rented public housing has had some deplorable results. Not that Dr Owen denies the benefits of a privately owned housing sector, but I would go as far as positively to welcome its growth. He is right, however, to question the degree of assistance given to house purchase; a lower ceiling ought to be imposed on mortgage relief.

The provision of the social services should be re-examined by the Alliance from this angle. On the one hand, we should be constantly raising the lowest incomes, following the populist approach of Haseler and Eden; on the other hand, we should be increasing the co-operative element, a field in which Robert Oakeshott and Lord Young have been leaders. I stress their names not only to give them their due but also because they are both active supporters of the Alliance, and therefore advance along co-operative lines for the social services would be in accord with influential thinking in the movement.

The two developments which have impressed Robert Oakeshott, Michael Young and myself are the Lagun-Aro, associated with the Mondragon co-operatives in Spain, and the development at Bologna. There are no doubt many others which should also be examined.

The Lagun-Aro was founded because when the Mondragon industrial co-operatives were set up it was found that under existing Spanish law the members, being ranked as self-employed, were excluded from many of the provisions of the Spanish national social services. Therefore, no doubt to some extent also inspired by Basque national feelings and suspicion of the central Franco government, Mondragon set about running its own social services. These now include family allowances, disablement benefit, pensions, health care, compensation for temporary loss of earnings due to absence from work, temporary unemployment benefit, death benefits and dowries. The Lagun-Aro is of particular importance today in Britain not only because of some of the ideology behind it but also because it illustrates one way in which to deal with the faults which have grown up in the administration of our services.

What was apparent to anyone who looked around or had the smallest smattering of history has now become accepted — as is so often the case in the wake of the earnest statistics collecting of researchers, those experts in teaching grandmothers to suck eggs. Any operation which is so large that it is isolated from internal or external scrutiny and which is financed by public money will grow inefficient and extravagant. As Robert Oakeshott points out, such operations swing out of control in two areas: 'their own internal operations, because of the enormous numbers of staff employed, and the consumption of their benefits which will be increasingly abused'.*

Lagun-Aro serves a population of around 22,000 — that is to say, a local community sufficiently large to support its own services and sufficiently small to ensure that it is under the constant scrutiny of the members who subscribe to it. Its ratio of expenses to benefits is far better than its state equivalents and superior even to such private contractors as BUPA. It gets its money by means of a combination of fixed contributions and contributions raised according to the members' salaries. It is itself 'decentralized'; committees are elected from among the co-operatives concerned: through the General Assembly these committees fix the rates.

The first point is that the mere fact that the workers are in control, and *feel* themselves to be in control, of their own scheme sharply diminishes abuse. Temporary absence from the co-ops through sickness is half of that in other businesses whose workers receive state benefits. Second, the medical care operation is paid for out of the fixed portion of the contribution. It pays for hospital treatment as well as the services of doctors and the medicines prescribed. But while it pays 100 per cent of hospital fees, the patients contribute to other expenditure. If a particular committee under-spends, its members may be entitled to a rebate. Though up to now the Lagun-Aro has relied on outside medical

* In *Lagun-Aro . . .*, London: Job Ownership Limited, 1982.

resources, it has recently built a small hospital of its own. Third, as far as unemployment is concerned, the payments are made from the variable part of the contributions. In 1981 members contributed 4.25 per cent of their net disposable income. As the co-ops try to avoid unemployment by encouraging well-employed co-ops to take on under-employed members, and as up to now their economy has been buoyant, there have been only small calls on the unemployment fund — which is a fairly recent development. However, tough conditions are laid down in case the situation deteriorates; under these the co-ops are responsible for small numbers of redundancies and must reduce their distribution before unemployment benefit will be paid. For permanent disablement there is a separate programme, and Lagun-Aro also pays family allowances, death benefits and dowries. As far as pensions are concerned, those working in the co-ops must by law subscribe to the Mutualidad Autonomos, the state-run body for the self-employed. Lagun-Aro collects and forwards the minimum subscription but in addition has decided to run its own supplementary pension scheme.

This very brief outline can be supplemented by reference to Robert Oakeshott's paper. What I want to emphasize is that the services provided by Britain's social insurance scheme can be made more democratic, and some at least of the problems of inadequate finance can be met, by applying local co-operative principles to it.

The Bologna type of social service, as explained to Robert Oakeshott, Michael Young and myself on a visit there in 1982 and as expounded by Michael in an article for *New Society*,* works in conjunction with national or community services. It may thus provide a more practical starting-point. It has always seemed to me that our social services suffer from the handicap of treating recipients as passive clients. Particularly in the personal services to the old, the disabled and so on. I believe that to be a severe drawback. It does people no good to be handled as vegetables so long as they are capable of playing some more active part — indeed, it is well known that, for some, senility is hastened once they are no longer required to work. Further, money for the

* 'Social work Bolognese', *New Society*, 19 August 1982.

services will always be short and efficiency always desirable — efficiency which can be improved once the social worker and the client both have some say in their running.

The Co-operativa assistenza domiciliare infanzia, anziani infermi of Bologna is a co-operative which offers assistance to both private and public clients. Just as in Britain some local authorities are hiving off such operations as refuse collections to outside contractors, so some northern Italian local authorities employ co-operatives of social workers. Old or disabled people, families who are in difficulty over bringing up their children, go first to the social work department of the local authority, which can remain quite small, for it simply recommends clients to appropriate social work co-operatives. Each client then to some extent becomes a member of the co-operative and can share in its direction and decisions; he or she also takes a share of the profit.

We were greatly impressed by an old folk's club in one of the poorer parts of Bologna, run very largely by the old people themselves. For instance, on the night we were there the bar was being operated entirely by the old-age pensioners. Although it sells drink at prices slightly lower than those of the neighbouring café, it makes a profit, which returns to the club and the co-operative members. The advantages of this are obvious. Opposition to such structural changes here would surely come only from the bureaucrats and paternalists, from those who felt that their jobs were threatened or, in this case, from the teetotal lobby. A variety of services is provided by these methods; the fact that the co-operatives are welcomed and are efficient is shown by their spread over Italy.

As leading members of the SDP have already advocated that membership of the governing bodies of hospitals, for example, should be extended to representatives of the community, it should be easy to take this further step, which would also chime in well with the desire of the Alliance to decentralize. I stress again that just as structural change is needed in politics and industry, so it is also needed in the social services. We must not think of reform in the terms only of the present system, merely attempting to 'decentralize' from the centre or to spread existing institutions within the same framework. We have to work upwards, starting from what individuals, local groups or communities can do for themselves. We have to mobilize local aspirations or the common will to promote the common good of various groups, so that it can be expressed in ways that are not, in the formal British sense, purely political.

In this restructuring of the social services there should be an important role for voluntary societies. Like everything else in Britain, they have tended lately to become more dependent on a centralized bureaucracy. But they are maintained largely by the local work of hundreds of groups, usually composed of dedicated women, who raise the money and often perform the chores. The work of such groups is inadequately recognized. Every week in local papers there are notices of meetings, bazaars, functions, all the product of such devoted work, especially work connected with money-raising; Mrs Williams draws attention in *Politics is for People* to the success of the adult literacy campaign. A stronger bond between local social work and the voluntary societies should be much in line with SDP thinking. Such societies are already in being; they make little or no demand on the Exchequer and could be used to launch a new departure in social work.

In the social services, as in local government and in industry, the state should, wherever possible, make available any necessary finance without taking direct responsibility for management. British agriculture has been relatively successful because the Government, while providing money, has not attempted to manage farms. Direct management by public authorities too often results in monopoly, inefficiency and stagnation.

7

Education

During their first spell of power or influence I do not see much need for the Alliance to spend a great deal of time on primary education. That is not because it is perfect but because there are other and more pressing needs, and once again the way to improve primary education is to raise the incomes of the poor and of the poorer communities.

One proposed change is to institute a system of vouchers. The introduction of vouchers would promote three desirable developments: it would give parents more choice; it would encourage schools to provide a better education; and it might relieve the Exchequer of some expenditure. But I am not convinced that at present all parents would make wise choices or, indeed, would know how to choose at all so far as primary education is concerned. I do not entirely share Arthur Seldon's optimism about this. Parents are not at present accustomed to making this sort of choice. The general atmosphere of British life would have to be changed to make such choices familiar, and this would at least take time. Now parents might well be swayed by considerations other than the pursuit of educational excellence. Good schools which were pioneering unfashionable methods might be starved of pupils. But the most serious drawback would be that the 'worst' schools would become 'worse' still through the siphoning off of their best potential pupils. These schools tend to be in the poorest communities — that is to say, those communities which particularly need help. So at least until we achieve greater equality of individuals and communities I would suggest that vouchers should be used only as a supplement to direct financing in the later stages of education. Dr Boyson is obviously right in telling us that high expenditure will not guarantee good education. Certainly, luxurious school buildings will no more make a scholar than fine golf clubs will a golfer. But some incentive to persuade good teachers to accept jobs in the poorer areas is necessary.

In an age in which technology is of increasing importance it is no doubt essential to support and extend secondary, technical and scientific education and the teaching of languages. But the principal shortcoming of the British educational system at present, it seems to me, is that many pupils emerge with little understanding of the ways of their country. Many will doubtless want to amend or reject its ways — but they should at least understand them. Some knowledge of our history and of our political methods and a handful of general moral principles provide a framework that is essential if common bonds are to be maintained and certain common goals pursued. Further, members of a democratic society which aims to offer wider choices for all must be taught how to make judgements. This is of crucial importance when television and the press can impose fashions, exploit weaknesses and titillate an appetite for violence. Advertising, with its constant stimulation of all sorts of demand, good and bad, can damage a country whose citizens have not been taught to discriminate. Another deficiency of our educational system seems to me to be the failure to teach all children the skills that they must use in later life — cooking, elementary maintenance of cars and houses, how to keep accounts and so on. When these skills are taught, it is often with the aid of equipment that is unnecessarily sophisticated and in a somewhat rarefied atmosphere. Few children will ever have access in later life to cookery, carpentry or engineering equipment to match that provided by most schools.

Dr Mary Warnock, in her admirable short book *Education: the Way Ahead*,* begins her chapter on comprehensive schools with the words: 'It is by what they teach that schools must be judged.' In Parliament most education debates are about the financing or organization of education — indeed, this is necessarily so, since the Department of Education does not lay down directly and precisely what shall be taught. Such latitude is surely right. Dr Warnock sets out what might be the content of a common cur-

---

* *Education, The Way Ahead*, Mainstream Book Club, Blackwell, 1979.

riculum, but while allowing for considerable flexibility, especially over the matter of which subjects should be examined, she also suggests that some subjects might be contracted out to special summer schools designed to meet the needs of those who wish to pursue them.

The question of who decides what should be taught raises two other issues: the training of teachers and the future of the Department of Education. The difficulty that I have come across in connection with teacher training is that teaching is not a seamless robe. Many good teachers, particularly of small children, have had no formal training. Teachers today devote much time to administration; this suits some but frustrates others. Brilliant teachers, certainly at the secondary and tertiary levels, conform to no pattern and have little in common except perhaps wholehearted commitment to their subjects. Further, their pupils may not, at the time, appreciate how good they are. We can no doubt turn out an adequate number of adequate teachers through teachers' training colleges, but we cannot command the required number of brilliant teachers when we want them. Teaching is to some extent a vocation or art. I do not think that in the short term the Alliance can do more than perhaps encourage the production of a common curriculum as a guide, provide further training for teachers and stress the need for instruction in analysis, in the world around us and in the making of judgements.

If education is to be left largely to local authorities, do we need a Ministry of Education? Mr Peter Hordern has convincingly raised questions about the need for such a Ministry.* A common outline curriculum could be drawn up by a meeting of, say, teachers, parents, local authorities and directly elected representatives. The provision of educational finance could be dealt with by the Treasury. I think there is a case for examining the need for a Ministry of Education, but any decision must lie in the future, and in any case we should require a Minister of Education to initiate the changes.

As far as the private schools are concerned, since I share the view of many members of the SDP that the private and public schools should work more closely together, I applaud the suggestion

* In 'Public Servants under Public Scrutiny', *Daily Telegraph*, 14 October 1981.

made in its Green Paper No. 4* that private boarding schools should provide places for state-supported boarders. I would certainly like to see the private sector retained.

I come now to the position of children of 15—16 and over. The school-leaving age was raised before we had provided adequately for the extra year of education or thought out the implications of the change. Many children are bored by their last year at school. The rate of truancy in some schools is very high. Girls particularly feel they have reached physical maturity while they are still treated as schoolchildren. They may be naive in many ways, nevertheless they want to get out into the adult world and earn money. The Alliance should consider what changes are needed in the final years of secondary education and in the transition period from secondary to tertiary education.

It is at this point, the end of secondary education and the move either to work or to tertiary education, that vouchers may be appropriate. The people concerned will by this time have developed views of their own: parents will have had some experience of education. Vouchers could be used for a further period at a secondary school, or for voluntary service, or for experience at work outside school. Vouchers too might be used to finance, at least in part, undergraduate tertiary education.

If we are to encourage more children to go on to tertiary education, we must provide a more interesting and varied spread, one which can be contained within the present span of education time (which, indeed, for many might be reduced even now). For the time being the school-leaving age should be left where it is — though when the changes in incomes and educational methods and attitudes that I recommend have taken effect, I should like to see discretion left, within a year or two, as to when particular children should finish.

At this stage in education three considerations are important: first, every child should be able to gain some experience of life outside education before going on to tertiary schools or colleges; secondly, the needs of special categories of children (for example, the musically talented) should be catered for; thirdly, practical training should be offered. And, of course, I attach great importance

* *Foundations for the Future: An Education and Training Policy.*

to continuous education in morals, politics and the many aspects of life in Britain. Vouchers should be offered to every child who wants to continue after secondary education to enable him or her both to spend a year in industry, voluntary service or other occupation and then to go on to the type of further education which he or she favours. I would like to see the binary system abandoned but apprenticeships and practical training tied in more closely with education.

Great emphasis is placed now on technical training. We are told that Britain's troubles are attributable to the low esteem in which industry and the men who work in it are held and to the lack of engineers and technicians, especially in new fields which have opened up, such as electronics. I wholly agree with the first of these sentiments, but we must be careful that in a laudable effort to boost the wealth producers we do not make fresh mistakes. Oxbridge is undoubtedly the fortress of traditional British educational attitudes, yet our oldest universities (particularly perhaps Cambridge) have also been in the van of British scientific discovery. Oxbridge attitudes may be blamed for our failure to exploit our discoveries. They may have rated technology and development too low. But universities have a special responsibility for pure research, for pushing forward the frontiers of knowledge. Secondly, if the humanities, arts and law are rated too highly, in both the older English and the Scottish universities they have been the training ground for public service. They have inculcated a devotion to the public weal which is both admirable and highly practical. Without it Britain would have lost much of her virtue. The trouble is that the sphere of activity to which training in the humanities was formerly particularly relevant has grown so large that it is no longer a hub around which our society revolves. It has become a vested interest on its own. If we are to pin our further education on universities rather than on a system of specialist institutions such as France's Grands Ecoles (which is a feasible alternative), we must understand and foster the essential characteristic of universities, which is that they both embrace a wide spectrum of subjects and teach and promote all these subjects within a general education in civilization, morality and judgement. We must be careful not to destroy the very essence of the university.

I doubt if we should extend university education at present. In an ideal society every young man and woman would benefit from it, and we must keep this ideal before us, but at present there are probably as many students at universities who should not be there as there are people of university age who should be there but cannot get places. And there are more urgent calls on the money available. Our first aim should be to extend practical training — training of all kinds. No doubt we require more highly skilled electronic engineers and their like. But as technology advances, it displaces not only unskilled but skilled labour too. It has been a commonplace for many years that the richer countries require more services and that not all those services are highly skilled. There is a growing demand for odd-job men and women of all kinds, from baby-sitters and gardeners to those who can carry out fairly simple repairs on plumbing, motor cars and television sets. What is needed is a reformed system of practical apprenticeships in which the apprentices work in industry but are also offered simultaneous general courses. The success of adult education and the Open University is evidence of the appetite for such courses.

The independent University of Buckingham has shown that shorter courses (say, of two years) can turn out graduates just as well qualified as many who have studied for three or four years. This being so, there seems to be no reason why a three-year training should not include both practical training and some continuation of general education. Many technical colleges and polytechniques have adopted this approach, which integrates them more closely with the work that their graduates will eventually seek. An RAF station in my constituency offers local boys and girls training in cookery and vehicle maintenance; this seems highly desirable, especially if it can be coupled with general classes.

While I believe that it would be beneficial for the children — and, indeed, for the educational system and the teachers, if not for educational bureaucrats — if some experiments were to be carried out with vouchers in the later stages of secondary education and if wide use were made of vouchers to encourage more pupils to take up tertiary education, I do not believe that vouchers could wholly finance any step forward in education. The Alliance, in my view, should insist that direct grants must be made to specialized schools, to colleges and, particularly, to universities. In the case of the latter the expenses of research into electronics and bio-technology, for instance, are very high. Should these grants continue to be made, as at present, or does the system need revision? At the moment, at least in the universities with which I am familiar, a very small part of the finance of scientific research comes from university funds. The greatest part comes from the University Grants Committee (UGC) and the Research Councils, which supply nearly two-thirds of the grants. This has its dangers: it means, among other things, that scientific research is highly centralized. Universities must seek to please those bodies. It could be argued that too much money has been spent on astronomy and its kindred studies. Further, the UGC has been criticized for being too much influenced by Oxbridge and for responding too little to the more technically inclined universities such as Aston and Salford. It is not necessary to accept such criticisms in full to be rather alarmed at the power that the UGC wields. To my mind, the Alliance, while retaining a body which can oversee the whole tertiary system – thereby departing from the binary division, which, as I have urged, should be demolished – must press that some grants for research (and, indeed, other purposes) are made direct to universities, to be used at their discretion. The relationship between the universities and industry must remain close: but it would be dangerous for the former to depend on industry for a greater proportion of their funds than at present.

When Mrs Shirley Williams was at the Department of Education an interesting paper was issued to universities. It offered the following suggestions for comment and discussion:

1. the reduction or removal of student grant aid, coupled with a system of loans;
2. a similar policy at the postgraduate level only;
3. a more restrictive policy as regards the admission of overseas students;
4. the requirement that grant-aided students should enter specified kinds of employment for a period after graduation, which might have the effect of reducing applications;

5. the greater use of part-time and correspondence courses as alternatives to full-time courses;
6. the possibility that the most able should have the opportunity to complete a degree course in two years;
7. the possibility that some students should proceed not to the customary three-year course but to a different course lasting only two years and leading to a different qualification;
8. the insertion of a period between school and university which would give school-leavers a better opportunity to formulate their views about whether or not they wished to proceed to some form of higher education;
9. the more intensive use of buildings and equipment, including perhaps the reorganization of the academic year;
10. more sharing of facilities between adjacent institutions;
11. more home-based students;
12. the development of Student Housing Associations and other forms of loan-financed provision for student residences;
13. some further increase in student/staff ratios.

At the time that these points were put forward the universities were walking very tall and were sure of their position in the wake of the Robbins Report.* They were unwise to treat the paper as cavalierly as most of them did. Neither Mrs Williams nor I would approve of all of the suggestions, but some are still pertinent. I quote them to illustrate that an educational policy along the lines that I have indicated would not be a totally new departure for the SDP at least. Indeed, I think that it would fit in with the party's desire to decentralize and to introduce more democracy at all levels. It would also be consonant with the desire of parents and of adolescents, as they get richer, to have more say in educational issues and to be offered more diversity. The Alliance might well look on the points as an agenda for further discussion.

In addition to considering these questions, it is time for the universities to consider the contribution that they can make to a more efficient Civil Service. They are still the main producer of senior civil servants, who are still generalists. To some extent

* *Higher Education*, Cmnd 2134, London: HMSO, 1963.

Litterae Humaniores, the Moral Tripos and the Humanities of the Scottish universities are courses aimed particularly at providing able and disinterested public servants with a wide perspective. Certainly, such people are still needed, though more in politics now than in the bureaucracies. But today there is also a need for technically qualified civil servants, as Lord Crowther-Hunt and others on the Fulton Committee argued.* The Grands Ecoles provide France with a superior service. I do not think that at present these schools should be duplicated here, but I would like to see in the universities courses similar to some that they run and perhaps some colleges or even whole small universities modelled upon them.

When it comes to a discussion of how education is to be paid for, the issues are in some respects similar to those raised by the funding of medicine. Both education and health care affect individuals, particularly children who cannot be left to make their own choices. Both are important to the opportunities that will be presented to the individual in later life. Both are becoming more complex. Public education however is, to my mind, much more open to criticism than the NHS, which may be administratively top-heavy but on the whole has performed well. In education the difference between the richer and poorer districts is very obvious. The results of many, though by no means all, state schools are inferior, at least in the secondary stage, to those of most private schools, no doubt largely because of the higher incomes of the families from which their children are drawn. One priority of the Alliance should be to improve the education offered in the poorer districts and to offer more choice where that is possible. Not only is it essential to raise incomes; it is also vital to choose a scheme by which parents can exercise more influence. Here the use of vouchers seems an obvious course. Parents would be given vouchers which could be used only to pay for education, but at the school of their choice. Decisions about the education of their children do not beset parents at moments of stress, as do decisions about medical treatment. At present I would confine vouchers to secondary education only, and then for only part of the cost. In fixing their values I would discriminate positively in favour of the poor.

* *The Civil Service*, Cmnd 3638, London: HMSO, 1968.

Further, as an immediate step the Alliance should step up such discrimination under the present system, reserving more money for schools in poorer areas.

I come now to the contentious matter of loans. Since giving the cleverest pupils a chance to gain further education in universities and colleges is clearly 'elitist' — that word of terrible connotation for the left — you would think that consistent socialists would at least maintain that the elite should repay to the general taxpayers the cost of the training which has enabled them to earn higher salaries. Once at Trinity College, Dublin, I was asked why the peasants of Connemara should pay for any part of the further education of the rich Dublin bourgeois. There are two arguments against loans: first, they may deter some suitable candidates from embarking on higher education because they will not want to incur debts; secondly, there is an element of 'public good' about all education. A country should be pleasanter to live in and more prosperous, and its affairs should be better managed, if it has a high proportion of well-educated citizens. A third argument, that young men and women should not be asked to start on life burdened with debt, nor forced to take better-paid jobs to discharge it, can be met by ensuring that repayment of a loan (which, presumably, would be by way of taxation) does not begin until a certain level of salary has been reached. The first argument may well be valid in regard to working-class families, and since it is those who already gain least from higher education (as they are unable to make use of it or reluctant to encourage their children to consider it), it is a serious argument. At present I believe that loans should be introduced only for postgraduates; otherwise the present system of grants, perhaps topped up by loans, should continue for undergraduates in tertiary education. I see no reason why such a move towards greater equality as asking postgraduates to contribute to what must be an advantage for them should affront Liberals or Social Democrats. Loans have long been common in countries ruled by social democratic governments. When the crucial reform of raising lower incomes had been achieved and we were in a position to see how the experiment with postgraduates had fared, the matter could be examined again.

8

Law and Order

The question which must be asked about law and order seems simple and obvious: how do we reduce murder, assault and robbery? It is worth putting it at the head of the chapter. Serious as may be fraud, trouble at football matches, breaches of regulations and innumerable other offences, these are of secondary importance compared with the protection of the citizen going about his or her lawful occasions.

The history of crime in Britain is relevant to any proposals for handling it. In the late eighteenth and early nineteenth centuries in England, particularly in London, violence was rife. The Gordon riots were merely a peculiarly fierce eruption of the lawlessness which was endemic. How far this was true of other, and particularly of smaller, cities seems doubtful. The Porteous mob in Edinburgh was certainly ferocious. But although dozens of crimes, many of them petty, were rewarded with the death penalty in Scotland (as in England), years would pass with no hangings in Edinburgh (many convicts, of course, escaped). Until the enterprise of Deacon Brodie, who combined public service with burglary, the burghers of Edinburgh left the keys of their apartments on hooks outside their front doors. It is worth noting that the comparative absence of assault and burglary has been attributed to the great number of caddies or street porters who hung about the capital, well versed in the ways of its inhabitants, ready to do errands of every kind and, in spite of dire poverty, remarkably law-abiding. The caddy-on-the-beat seems to have deterred many a criminal. Towards the end of the nineteenth century, it seems, crime declined throughout Britain. Such statistics as exist, after due allowance for their inadequacy and changes in the law, seem to show that for about seventy years Britain was a relatively law-abiding country so far as assault and robbery are concerned.

I suspect that the statistics need to be qualified. My recollection is that in the 1920s Dundee was a fairly violent town, at least on Saturday nights. Drunken fights on the common stairs, the knocking about of wives and such like, not being much reported to the police, were probably not included in the statistics of crime. But it is true that much crime was due to drink; there was less organized burglary, and during the day passers-by were safe in streets and tenements. In 1955 Professor Geoffrey Gorer could write in *Explaining the English Character*: 'In public today the English are certainly the most peaceful, gentle, courteous and orderly population that the civilized world has ever seen. . . . you hardly ever see a fight in a bar. . . . football crowds are as orderly as church meetings. . . .' This must now read very queerly to Continental sufferers from English football visitors.

It is during the 1970s, according to the statistics, that crime has grown so steeply. If I have the history right, it would indeed seem that the modern rise in crime is not due primarily to poverty, which is steadily declining. Even shoplifting seems to be the temptation of the comparatively well off. Greed, rather than want, seems to be the spur. Nor does bad housing account for violence. The slums of the nineteenth and early twentieth century were appalling. In the 1970s it was often in new housing estates that vandalism and mugging flourished. Nor is it anything to do with a dearth of social services, which have grown along with crime. In Sweden, as in Britain, crime has risen steeply in the last twenty-five years, despite an all pervading welfare state. In 1955, 225,000 offences against the Swedish Penal Code were known to the police; in 1979 the corresponding figure was nearly 700,000. The Swedish experience also discounts the view that violence is necessarily associated with immigrants.*

The causes of the rise of modern crime do not seem to me difficult to find. It is the dissolution not so much of religious belief itself — though that undoubtedly contributes — but of the responsibility and rectitude which arose from our Christian and

---

* I am indebted to Mr Christie Davies's article in *Policy Review*, Winter 1982, for much of the foregoing information.

Greek heritage, and the slackening of family and class ties, that have weakened personal morality. Formerly, men and women may have fought when drunk, but when sober they did not pretend that such conduct was excusable or anyone else's fault but their own. The support of the family, the neighbourhood, their class, helped to prop up potential delinquents or to shame them if they succumbed. Unemployment, though not now accompanied by acute poverty, leaves young men and women with time on their hands. Modern living conditions often offer them nowhere to go. In as respectable and as comparatively prosperous a town as Lerwick in Shetland, where the climate is hardly conducive to dawdling in the dusk, the doors of closed shops used to be filled with groups of well-behaved and well-dressed youngsters sitting on the cold stone because, as they told me, they had nowhere else to go. Yet social workers, youth organizations, churches and church halls abounded — let alone their own homes. The raising of the school-leaving age — before we had any clear idea how children who already considered themselves to be adults were to spend their last year at schools which bored them — did not help. Truancy became normal in some classes.

Step by step with the decline in personal, family and neighbourhood responsibility went the growth of the welfare services, services which expressly precluded participation, services which treated their clients rather in the way that the kindest owners treat their animals, services which did not depend on natural ties or affection. So the whole philosophy of non-responsibility flourished, with its accompanying jargon. It was in the late 1960s that the bureaucratic state fastened upon us.

The law became detached from morality. It is, of course, true that many sins are not, and should not be regarded as, crimes. But the creation of a vast body of crimes which are not sins is a new phenomenon. As Lord Devlin pointed out in *The Enforcement of Morals*,* one result of severing the connection between crime and immorality is that the law 'frequently does not care whether it catches the actual offender or not'. Owners of goods are often made absolutely liable for what happens to the goods while they

---

* New York: Oxford University Press, 1965.

are under their control, even if they are in no way responsible for interferences with them.

The law thus becomes a matter of convenience. And it is the Government (that is, the party in power), with its bureaucrats, which decides what is convenient. Of course, some decisions of convenience (for example, that we should all drive on the same side of the road) are essential, but when we are trapped in a vast mesh of regulations, some of which seem absurd to most people, the law itself is cut from its mooring in morality and brought into disrepute. I sympathize with people who feel a positive duty to break some regulations every day. The only restraint is fear of penalty. If the chances of being caught are small, well, why not commit the crime?

To this gelding of the law modern fashions have yoked two further restraints that tend to weaken its impact. One of these is the removal of the police from the community. The police force has been bureaucratized, mounted in motor cars, pinned behind desks and occupied with the filling of forms and reports. Every year Parliament loads more duties upon it. (Has it not now even got to make sure we wear seat belts?) There has been talk of getting the constable back on the beat. I can only say that in the street where I live, which has its quota of burglaries and assaults, I have never, over the last six years, seen a policeman on foot. The other fashion is television, which demands spectacle — violent spectacle is particularly acceptable. The newspapers are open to the same criticism. People are so inured to violence — or at least to shouting, marching, would-be intimidation and exaggeration of personal differences — that they come to think there is nothing wrong with it, that reason and honest dealing have no place.

Add to all this the ugliness and brutality of modern architecture and I find it no wonder that crime increases. Decency, respect for other people, unselfishness can thrive only when people like each other, when they live in a humane and cheerful environment, when attempts to produce beautiful artefacts please the heart even when they are despised by the art pundits. Flowers, ornaments, best dresses, chosen by themselves and proudly displayed as their own possessions, gladden people. The concrete desert, the large matchbox blocks of flats, the glowering mass which frowns like a Kremlin on the individual foment a sour and discontented generation — a generation ripe for crime. No one has much respect for public property, which becomes a testing-ground for vandals.

If my diagnosis is right, law and order must start with education — not an original conclusion but perhaps true nonetheless. The difficulty is that the prevention of crime is not a sufficient reason for converting people to Christianity or, indeed, any morality. If you do not accept certain standards, to announce that you do so that others may be deterred from violence is to sound a cynical note. Nevertheless, I can hardly believe — though successive Russian Governments and Hitler's Reich are powerful arguments against me — that men have entirely lost the desires and beliefs that have survived in Western Europe since Greece. On the contrary, it is obvious that, for a vast majority of people at most times, the old beliefs, the desire for beauty and laughter and happiness and jolly parties persists. If we look to teachers to assist in reducing the amount of crime, the process must probably start at the universities. There is a great need to reinstate the ideals, if not the exact curricula, of Greats, the Humanities and the Moral Tripos for a variety of reasons concerned with running a better country.

In the field of morals too decentralization, smaller units, are as necessary as in government or industry, and for the same reason — the reinstatement of personality. We should learn the lesson of old Edinburgh, and indeed of some modern teachers, that in every community a presence standing on the side of order is a useful cement and deterrent. There is no substitute for the local constable, knowing his neighbourhood, walking about it at all times of day and night. As with other professions, the nine-to-five stint has killed the effectiveness of the police. I am inclined to think too that the police should be under local control, though this has drawbacks. The police, in turn, must be backed by parents and neighbours. The old-fashioned busybody and the interfering aunt have their place.

I return now to where I started. This recipe for law and order is designed to stop assaults, burglary, crimes against persons and property. It cannot cover the huge field in which the police are now supposed to operate, nor can it cope by itself with organized terrorism (though I suspect it would make a substantial contribution to its elimination). To enable them to deal with what I think are their main tasks, I believe that we must relieve the police of certain duties. First, the police are obliged to enforce far too many regulations. The repeal of some already in existence and the reduction of others would mean that fewer forms and returns were required. Secondly, the supervision of activities in which people put themselves at risk absorbs a disproportionate amount of the time and energy of the police. I reiterate that the duty of the police is to see that I can go about my normal business and may live in peace, not to enable me to embark on risky undertakings which I undertake at my peril. The conduct of football matches at some stadiums has now reached a stage where everyone knows that if you attend them, you may be in trouble. They have ceased to be part of normal life. The football clubs should be told that if they want order at their matches, they must hire private enforcement officers. Similarly, I cannot see why the courts and the police should waste their time dealing with gambling or pornography. If you want to gamble, you should take the risks, and if you lose your money, too bad. It may be that we should impose stiff taxes on organized gambling, but otherwise *caveat emptor* should apply. I may be asked why if pubs need a licence, gambling houses should not. The answer is that the denizens of pubs may be a nuisance. Unless the pub is conducted in an orderly fashion, drunks may debauch the neighbourhood. But gamblers, as far as I know, are eminently quiet and law-abiding. As for demonstrations, they should be confined to areas like Hyde Park. I can see no justification for sending hundreds of police to patrol the West End of London on a Sunday morning. These demonstrations have nothing to do with free speech. They are ineffective as a lobby. They interfere with the freedom of others and so transgress Mills's dictum about the limits of freedom.

Special squads are required to fight terrorism and large-scale organized crime. The policeman required for such work may be different from the policeman on the beat; the career structure for such technically proficient agents may differ from that which the local constable can expect. But the local constable is the lynch-pin of the force, and I am convinced that the local police, constantly on the beat, knowledgeable about their area and supported by the local community are the key to order. To reinstate the police force in the community should be an early task for the Alliance.

When it comes to the law itself, the Alliance will have to take longer to carry out the reforms which I believe to be very necessary. As far as the protection of the rights of the citizen by civil law is concerned, the system has become too expensive and too slow. Legal aid will continue to lead to serious injustices as long as a successful litigant can be left with the costs of an action or a litigant who is in fact wealthy is able to succeed in divesting himself for the purposes of the action. Legal aid too, so some judges tell us, not only encourages unnecessary litigation but also causes it to be unduly prolonged. Simpler and cheaper justice is obviously desirable. Yet we are threatened with the kind of legal bonanza which has broken out in the USA, where case and counter-case are brought, often resulting in very high damages. Many doctors and other professional men and women are reluctant to try new techniques for fear of the heavy damages which may be awarded against them if they fail. Insurance can be a safeguard, but that is now becoming very expensive.

It seems to me that if we are both to provide simpler and more generally available remedies in civil actions and to simplify the criminal law, we should start with the legal profession itself. It remains a closed shop, meriting all the criticisms aimed at industrial closed shops. I have never been able to understand why a defendant or litigant should not be entitled to be represented by a person of his or her choice, whether legally trained or not. The reservation of certain courts to certain classes of lawyer — indeed, the division of the profession into barristers or advocates and solicitors — seems to me difficult to support. Like other closed shops, the law is riddled with restrictive practices which are maintained to suit lawyers, not the public.

As far as the criminal law is concerned, the prisons are overcrowded, and the existing penalties do not appear to be effective deterrents. If we are to relieve the pressure on the prisons, we must increase the likelihood of being caught. That takes us back to the police on the beat. We must also make crime more difficult.

While we give grants for such improvements as insulation, we give no encouragement to the householder to install anti-burglar devices. Stolen cars are essential tools of criminals, yet car manufacturers still make their products childishly easy to steal. While it is difficult to think of punishments other than fines or imprisonment for the great bulk of offences, yet rather more imagination could be shown over penalties. Mr Jack Profumo, who has long experience of the East End of London, believes that the withdrawal of motor bicycle and motor car licences would be a deterrent to youths with a propensity for crime.

I have not dealt with the inner-city racial riots. This book is not intended to cover every aspect of policy. I have no very original ideas to contribute to the keeping of order in the inner cities. I agree with much of what Lord Scarman said in his report on Brixton,* but I believe that improved local government would certainly help to avoid future troubles. One cause of the riots has been the disastrous 'planning' by local authorities. I also believe that improved industrial relations and social services would help. The behaviour of the rioters on whom the blame must squarely rest has been compounded by some of the excuses trotted out by their supporters. Here again we come up against the need for a change in education. People in responsible posts, social workers among them, have shown an extraordinary failure to grasp the essentials of a satisfactory society.

* *A Report of the Enquiry into the Brixton Disturbances*, Cmnd 8427, London: HMSO, 1982.

International Relations

9

Foreign Policy

What are the principal aims of British foreign policy (and therefore of British defence policy)? They are, I would suggest, first to protect ourselves from Russian aggression. I know of no country except the USSR which is likely to involve us in a major war; if the USSR did not exist or was in democratic hands, our defence forces could be very small. Secondly, we have an interest in world prosperity. We are a nation dependent upon international trade. Thirdly, the success of the EEC, both political and economic, is a British interest. We also are ready to play a part in helping poorer nations in Asia, Africa and South America. How far the prosperity or unity of the Commonwealth should be a principal aim of Britain is for me an interesting question. Certainly, the Commonwealth has its value. In crises the white Commonwealth has proved a loyal and valuable ally, nor are the less obvious ties with the black and brown Commonwealth to be underrated. But the Commonwealth does not bulk large, I would have thought, in our foreign or defence policy — certainly not as large as it did before the war. Again, the Middle East is important to us, but we no longer have direct responsibilities there.

None of these aims can we achieve by ourselves. Most of the talk about British sovereignty is pedantry. For defence against the USSR we depend upon NATO, for our own well-being on international trade and agreements and on our membership of the EEC. Our main hope for helping Asia, Africa and South America lies in acting in concert with our allies.

There are two questions which require consideration in connection with our aims. One is our attitude towards the United Nations.

Of course, it should be British policy to try to improve the working of the UN as an instrument of international co-operation and peacekeeping, but can it be said to be a major British aim to strengthen the UN? Considering its extraordinary composition — as a heterogeneous collection of states ranging from countries no bigger than a biggish city to those the size of the USA, many of them dictatorships and many impoverished and unstable — the UN has done rather better than might have been expected. But this is very largely due to the Americans and, to a lesser extent, to the Western Europeans. The UN will remain a useful instrument for important purposes (for example, aid to poorer countries) just as long as the USA and the Western Europeans are prepared to pay for it and support it. I am afraid that the common international action, desire for collective security and increasing respect for international law which the founders of the League of Nations and their successors at the birth of the United Nations hoped would spread through the influence of these bodies has not extended very far.

In the 1930s many people thought that the strengthening of the League of Nations should be a prime aim of British foreign policy. Britain was still a leading world power. Her responsibilities were worldwide. It is partly a measure of her shrunken horizons that she must now leave the ordering of the world to others. But it is the overwhelming need to defend ourselves against the USSR that, to my mind, has relegated the UN to a secondary position. For in defence against the Soviet Union the UN is little help. It remains, however, a useful means of attaining certain objects of our foreign policy.

The other question which should be raised is this: is it a principal aim of Britain's foreign policy to spread freedom and democracy? My immediate response is no. If we remain at peace with the communist states, that is the most we can hope for. It is beyond our powers to convert dictatorships to democracy. Even if it were within our powers, in many parts of the world the attempt might lead to instability and war. Our attitude towards this issue is ambivalent. We join in the attempt to impose some sort of sanctions on the USSR over Afghanistan, then we agree to help her build a gas pipeline. There is a constant demand for sanctions of one sort or another on South Africa, yet worse tyrannies escape.

To answer this question we have to examine further what I take to be the principal aim of our policy — defence against the USSR. Marxism is an aggressive philosophy. Dictatorships are in any case notoriously apt to be aggressive. Wars have normally been caused not by free capitalist, small-government countries but by countries in the grip of powerful bureaucracies. Socialists are apt to ignore the fact that the pre-war Tory Government tried to appease Hitler because Mr Chamberlain and others in it loathed war. And one factor that contributed to Mr Chamberlain's loathing of war was his upbringing as a Birmingham businessman. It is not businessmen but those who believe in all-powerful states who are warlike. Russian Governments have committed every crime so far known to mankind, including the invasion and subjugation of their neighbours. As long, therefore, as the USSR remains in the thrall of an all-powerful state bureaucracy, which claims to be Marxist, she is a potential threat to world peace — and sometimes, as in the case of Afghanistan, an actual threat.

But that is not to say that the USSR will inevitably invade Europe. Huge armaments have always been accompanied by powerful military and bureaucracies with a certain professional momentum towards war. The Kaiser's War Office and army were an example of such a body — clearly attuned, in that case, to the idea of attacking France. The equivalent of the German General Staff now exists in the USSR. Even in the USA President Eisenhower warned us of the power of the Pentagon — but the Pentagon is encased in a democracy. However, dictators, general staffs, corporate states, provoke war only in the belief that they can win. Their belief may be ill-founded, but they must have some hope, however slender it is. As long as the West maintains anything like parity in nuclear weapons, the Russian Government knows that it cannot win. (I am told that the Russian War Office believes that it is possible for the world to survive a nuclear exchange but can only hope that the Kremlin is more sensible.) Let the West drop its guard, however, and the bias towards war will have no further restraint upon it. If it became likely that a Russian invasion of Western Europe would be successful (perhaps not even resisted), the pressures upon the Russian Government would be hard for it to resist. Would it not be fulfilling destiny, according to Marxist ideology? Would it not divert attention from its internal troubles and demonstrate at home and abroad that it was invincible? Would it not be rid of the disturbing effect of prosperity on its doorstep compared with misery in its own house? Would it not be able to lay its hands on all the riches of Western Europe? The temptation would be irresistible. A Russian government which did not take it might well be overthrown by its own war machine. It seems to me that the Russian Government is not actively bellicose now, but the situation in the USSR bears within it all the seeds of bellicosity. They would almost certainly germinate if the West ceased to hold an adequate nuclear deterrent.

The dilemma which Liberals face is explored in Michael Howard's *Law and the Liberal Conscience*.* They are prone to believe that democrats are invariably pacific; yet, as he says, 'they have repeatedly displayed a bellicose passion reminiscent of the worst years of the Wars of Religion.' While denouncing war, Liberals and socialists are prepared to fight fascism. The regarded the last war as a 'just' war. If so, a war against the atrocities of communism would surely be equally just.

Apart from war by accident, the only situation in which I can foresee the USSR indulging in aggression against the West might be if her Government were threatened by serious internal revolt. This poses a dilemma. As long as Russia is ruled by tyranny which believes that its religion will eventually be enforced on mankind, as long, indeed, as she is in the hands of a bureaucracy whose ruling position depends on terror, she is a threat to world peace. I do not suppose that the leaders in the Kremlin believe any more passionately in Marxism than Whitehall believes in Christianity, but the point is that any dictatorship is apt to turn aggressive when threatened, and Marxism, lying at the back of the Russian rulers' minds, could be invoked to justify war. It must therefore be in the interest of Britain and of the West to see the Russian dictatorship overthrown, yet an attempt to overthrow it may itself provoke the USSR to go to war.

Dissidents from communist countries, not least the courageous and experienced dissidents from the USSR herself, often warn us

* London: Temple Smith, 1978, p. 131.

against thinking that we shall achieve anything by being nice to the dictators. On the whole, they do not believe that contact by trade and tourism will soften the communist regimes. I suspect that the wretched slaves in Siberia are deeply depressed by Western participation in the pipeline. We have often been told by the Russians themselves that the way to free them is to let their incompetent system decline until its inefficiency becomes insupportable. They no more believe in appeasement than did the anti-Nazi Germans.

I am convinced that we will get nowhere by being nice to the Russians or, indeed, to other communist dictatorships. I have grave doubts about the pipeline and the sales of wheat by the USA. Western policy *vis-à-vis* Russia is bedevilled by a disease which affects the West in general — the fear that if we don't grab what we can, someone else will get in front of us. So Western Governments and traders are usually all too ready to do business with the USSR, regardless of the long-term interests of their countries. Nevertheless, it is clear that the West is not going to take the initiative and risk war on behalf of the dissidents in Eastern Europe — Hungary established that. What the reaction of the West might be to war between communist states or to serious civil war in the East is more doubtful. Our main immediate aim should be to maintain peace by deterrence through the balance of power (or, as some would say, terror). For the present at least stability is a main objective in East–West relations. But this does not mean that we should not bargain very hard for some let-up in the appalling tyranny of communism. If we are to keep the Soviet economy going, we should demand better treatment for the dissidents.

Our second aim, world prosperity, is clear. We cannot lift ourselves out of the depression. Standards of living, employment, our ability to help the poorer countries, all these depend upon the revival of world trade. If world trade revives, then to avoid inflation we will have to devise a world monetary system.

This second aim is closely linked with the third: the success of the EEC, for we shall exert most influence on trade and finance as members of the EEC. If we are to remain in the EEC, as I believe we must, then we must try to make it work better, and try not as saboteurs but as partners (though I see no justification for our constant appeasement of the French — bad allies most of the time). We should at once join the monetary system. We should put forward positive proposals for improving the budgeting arrangements. We should propose that there should be further discussions within the EEC about its relationship with member countries, certain aspects of which I find unsatisfactory. Britain may do badly by the flow of funds within the community, but some of her so-called gains fill me with alarm. Euro-MPs and others anxious to boost the EEC frequently point to large grants made for this purpose or that. Some of these grants seem to me extremely ill-judged: sometimes they smack of bribery, and sometimes they are wrongly directed. If my experience in the North of Scotland is matched elsewhere in Europe, money is being wasted on a large scale. A proportion of it is our money, and in many cases we shall be left with liabilities to be met by future generations.

I would hope that the Alliance, with Mr Jenkins, a most distinguished ex-Secretary-General of the EEC among its leaders, would propose an agenda for discussions about its further development. On the political side, the proposal by the European Parliament that it should interest itself in Northern Ireland raises the question of European responsibility for troubled areas in the member countries. Any interference in Northern Ireland is likely to make things worse because of the existence of a small criminal minority dedicated to violence, a handful of people ready to use any excuse to justify their cause and persuade the much larger Roman Catholic minority that it has a grievance. Nevertheless, the hostile reaction to any suggestion that the EEC might have a part to play in troublesome matters involving not one member but two seems to me misguided. The British have not been so successful in their handling of Ireland that they can brush aside all offers of assistance. If the EEC lasts and expands to take in all Western Europe, it should devise some accepted rules for the handling of political disputes.

On the agenda too should be the control of expenditure. As I argue elsewhere, we are suffering in Britain from the divorce of taxation from government expenditure. Governments can commit large sums of money before the people who ultimately have to pay, through tax or inflation, are aware of what is happening. The European budget seems even further removed from the discipline of repercussions upon taxpayers. The growth of bureaucracy and of bureaucratic outlook that is so obvious in Britain has even more opportunities in Europe. Already travel expenses have caused a scandal. Salaries, perks, conferences, staff will all continue to proliferate unless checked.

Third, the biggest single factor which turns ordinary citizens against the EEC is its propensity to make irritating or positively objectionable regulations. All Governments too malleable to the demands of their bureaucrats are inclined this way. Some check needs to be imposed in Brussels as in London.

There is, then, the question of assistance to the regions. I should not complain: the Highlands and Islands have benefited considerably. When, however, I look at Palermo and contrast its poverty with the well-being of Stornoway I cannot believe that the EEC has its priorities right. It seems to me that something must be wrong not only with the decisions but also with the machinery for making them.

Nevertheless, the disappearance of the cloud which has lain over Europe for a thousand years — the plague of Western European wars, which has been so completely expunged that new generations do not even appreciate the boon of its dispersal — is alone worth any petty tribulations that the EEC may inflict.

When it comes to aid for poorer countries, the Alliance should stress to the limit of its ability the lessons of the last fifty years. The first essential is that countries to be aided must be in a position to use the aid. The enormous increase in wealth in the USA and Japan — not so long ago under-developed countries — was made possible by a stable political system, a reasonably impartial law, capitalism and the free market. Socialism of the kind that many developing countries favour, seen at its peak in the USSR and Cuba, guarantees poverty for the masses — though often alongside luxury for the dictators and their henchmen. I find it very difficult to see how aid will ever be given to the best advantage to poorer countries as long as it is sent largely to corrupt Governments with mistaken ideas about how growth can be achieved. But clearly such Governments have no incentive to give up their own power and the wealth which goes with it. Ex-colonial powers are embarrassed by their past. They are too frightened of being accused of neo-colonialism to bring much pressure to bear on the recipients of their bounty. I believe that often they are mistaken. The Alliance should perhaps examine the possibility of acting through countries which have never had imperial ambitions but have been commercially success-ful — Switzerland is the obvious paradigm.

Western democracies should not delude themselves that by giving aid they gain good will. If that were so, America would be far and away the most popular country in the world and the communists would be execrated throughout Africa and East Asia. We should remember the anecdote of Confucius quoted by the Indian Liberal Mr Masami in *Modern Liberalism*: * 'One man says to another, "Why do you dislike me so much? I have never done anything to help you." '

* F. Bolkestein (ed.), London: Elsevier, 1982, p. 170.

10

Defence

There is no reason in logic, economics or politics why Western Europe should not defend itself without the USA. But in the short run the American alliance is essential; the whole strategy of the free world depends on it. Further, the collaboration of Western Europe and the USA over defence bears fruit in all sorts of ways. So while ultimately Western Europe, though remaining an ally of the USA, must become wholly responsible for its own defence, that day is a long way off. NATO is, and should remain, at the centre of the defence policy of the Alliance. No distraction such as the Falklands affair should divert us.

I have explained our position *vis-à-vis* the USSR. I believe that were we to give up nuclear weapons unilaterally, the chances of a Russian invasion of Europe would very greatly increase. As long as we hold an adequate deterrent, I doubt if the USSR will make an attack. But I must say a word or two about who 'we' refers to and a word or two about 'adequate'.

I was opposed to the British independent nuclear deterrent. I could not conceive that we should ever use it on our own. To me the fact that NATO was backed by the American nuclear deterrent was enough. By insisting on our own we set a bad example to other nations, which might claim, with justice, that they too must have such a deterrent. It is possible that we weakened the Western Alliance, and we certainly deflected our resources from much more necessary conventional weapons.

I still think that there is force in these arguments, though they may be of declining relevance as more nations acquire a nuclear capability. However, I still find it hard to believe that any potential enemy could imagine that we would use British nuclear weapons without the agreement of the USA. Britain had to get out of the Suez Canal as soon as she turned against us. We have surely learned the lesson. Yet it is argued by some proponents of a British independent nuclear deterrent that in a world where soon many nations may possess nuclear weapons we must have some in our own hands for use in areas where our interests alone are threatened or attacked. Suppose, the argument runs, that the Argentinians had possessed nuclear weapons but we had not; we should then have been powerless to help the Falklands. There is some force in this. It may be that nuclear deterrence between the West and the USSR will have to be broadened into general deterrence.

Whatever one's view of the results of the proliferation of nuclear weapons, we have *Polaris*, and I believe that the Alliance is wise to accept the reality that we have a deterrent and have had for a long time. Like the SDP, I am prepared to accept cruise missiles if there is really a technical case for them — but not *Trident*. There is a danger that Governments and their general staffs will over-insure. There is no point in being able to wipe out the USSR ten times — once is enough. The cruise missile was originally offered to Europe by the Americans in the apparently mistaken belief that the Germans wanted it. I doubt if there was a case for the cruise programme, but it has gone a considerable way, and the SDP accept it, so I would advise the Alliance to acquiesce. If multilateral nuclear disarmament makes progress, there may come a time to offer its abandonment for some worthwhile counter-offer from the Russians.

Multilateral balanced nuclear disarmament must be to the advantage of the West. The great benefit that a programme to reduce nuclear arms would bring is an economic one. I do not believe that, in the absence of the sort of bellicosity which unilateralism might unleash, the mere size of the nuclear armouries contributes much to the danger of world war, so I am afraid that a reduction of nuclear arms, on either side of the Iron Curtain, would not contribute much to world peace. That an arsenal of nuclear weapons could no longer obliterate the protagonists in a war twenty times but could merely obliterate them would not do much to lessen the danger of extinction or to promote peace.

Nevertheless, it would have important economic effects, releasing resources for other purposes, which is the main argument for reduction in nuclear arms. Further, if the West could scale down its nuclear armoury, it should be able to increase its conventional strength. It is by increasing conventional strength in Europe that I believe Britain can improve her defences. If the Russians can quickly reach the Rhine or the Channel without recourse to nuclear arms, the West will be in a terrible dilemma. Should it risk a first strike? To me it is vital that there should be no possibility of over-running Western forces on the frontiers of Europe. This should remain the keystone of Alliance defence policy.

The Alliance must be ready to meet the arguments of the unilateralists. To those unilateralists who are pacifists I have nothing to say. It is reasonable and moral to maintain that all wars are evil and that we should never engage in them. This stance entails accepting the probability of Russian domination, the end of freedom, the rule of terror. If pacifism is to be a tenable view, its full consequences must be faced. Those who claim that the USSR would never annex further territories in Europe, would never interfere with the workings of democracy, are either deliberately blind or are deluded; nor is it morally defensible to allow other people to wield a deterrent on our behalf.

But most unilateralists are not pacifists. Some maintain that nuclear weapons are in a class of their own, so that while in certain circumstances conventional war may be justified, nuclear war could never be. I cannot accept this argument. Nuclear war, the destruction of the life and fabric of the planet itself, is infinitely horrible. But conventional war of the 1914—18 type seems to me horrible too, and there are other ways of wounding this planet besides the nuclear. I cannot believe that the difference in the degree of destruction makes high explosive moral and nuclear explosive immoral.

However, if my view of the morality of war is rejected, there is still the practical argument that for the West to maintain conventional forces while throwing away the nuclear shield would be futile. All an opponent with nuclear weapons would have to do would be to threaten their use or to use them, and the conventionally armed must surrender. The argument of Hiroshima is telling:

if the Japanese had possessed nuclear arms, the city would never have been obliterated.

There is then the argument of example, which is that if the West practises unilateral disarmament, the effect on the USSR will be such that she will be bound to follow. I see no reason to believe this. Nothing in the history of the Soviet Union, the doctrines which she professes or the nature of tyrannical bureaucracies provides any evidence to support this contention, and the evidence against it is overwhelming. The rabbit sets a splendid example of non-belligerence. The stoat eats it just the same. As to the effect of propaganda, it is difficult to get across to the Russian people any argument which their Government wishes to jam. It is, for me, impossible to believe that at present the Soviet Government will change its nature and its aims as a result of pressure from within — even if anti-nuclear protagonists were ever to succeed in making their case within the USSR.

It follows that I believe the declaration of nuclear-free zones by people who are not pacifists and will not face the probability of Russian aggression to be not only impractical but also immoral. I certainly do not believe that the Russians will respect unilateral announcements, nor do I believe it moral to shelter behind the nuclear weapons provided by other countries while attempting to contract out of any responsibility. This does not, I reiterate, mean that every country must possess nuclear arms, but it does mean that if any state relies upon NATO or any variant which retains a nuclear deterrent, it must take the responsibility that goes with sharing the benefits of the deterrent and must be prepared to make some contribution to it, such as the siting of nuclear weapons on its territory.

It is a fact of our lives that nuclear weapons exist. We cannot 'disinvent' them. Even if all existing weapons were to be destroyed, the capacity to make them would still exist. It may actually be safer that their existence is acknowledged than that they should be manufactured secretly in a world lulled by the belief that it has got rid of them. That they are an appalling addition to the world's means of destruction no one denies, but at present the best strategy — which, in fact, has maintained world peace for some thirty-eight years — is deterrence, coupled with constant attempts at multilateral disarmament and, as far as our ability permits, the removal of the causes of war.

In the next ten years the direction of danger may shift. It may arise not from possible Russian aggression but from the possession of nuclear weapons by other fanatical or aggressive states. If Iran or Iraq possessed such weapons, what could or would the world do to prevent their use? Nuclear-free zones would hardly help. In years to come we shall be forced to reconsider collective security, but at present the threat of annihilation is posed by the possibility that the arsenal of the USSR will be unleashed by the failure of Western deterrence.

Conclusion

The long-term aim of the Alliance must be a more diversified society with more equality of opportunity and more participation. I have described the policies which, it seems to me, are both feasible and desirable for the Alliance to pursue as those measures which will promote liberalism within the community and socialism without the state. In recent years we have relied too much upon the state and have paid too little attention to other forms of organization. Although the mould must be broken, that does not mean that we must jettison all the good that the mould has achieved; it does mean that we should seek new structures by which further progress can be made.

This points directly to decentralization — of decision-making, of government, of industry, of the social services and of education. But if the mainspring of our society is no longer to be the central government, then other sources of inspiration and power must be advanced. These sources must engage the active participation of individuals and must offer them greater opportunities. Yet opportunity is of use only to those who have the means to exploit it: hence the argument for a national minimum income, which would allow individuals to replace state services with services of their own choice. I accept, of course, that there will always be a section of the population that needs assistance from the public authorities, but this proportion should decline, and much of the assistance could be supplied by local bodies and co-operatives. Thus the ideals of the welfare society could be furthered without its present complication and *dirigisme*.

If the opportunities of the poor are to be enhanced by more

resources, we must build up from local communities. The sphere
of local government must be more carefully defined, but each
community should be encouraged to develop the way of life that
is best suited to it within that sphere. This will entail conferring
more powers of taxation on local authorities, so that they are
more directly compelled to match expenditure to income. An
immediate step towards this should be for local Alliance members
to identify the potentialities of their communities, so that they
are ready to take advantage of the central government aid which
will at first be necessary. They must also be ready to grasp the
opportunities which will be offered when the powers of the
central government are reduced.

To turn to reform of central government, I believe that the
major fault is the failure of the House of Commons to control
public expenditure on the public services. The reasons for this,
I think, are the size of these functions, the complexity of their
administration and the lack of incentives to promote efficiency
and economy. The remedy lies not only in reducing the size of
government but also in devising new methods, so that attention
can be directed to the main functions of government – defence,
the maintenance of law and order and certain services which are
largely public goods or which, at least for the present, should be
under public control. Among these I would include the National
Health Service (though it might well be supplemented by voluntary effort and insurance), the Post Office, certain forms of
transport and possibly an information channel on radio or TV.

I do not believe that we should set up new authorities or layers
of government to try to offset the trouble caused by unsound
structures. For instance, though well-intentioned, I consider that
the extension of the powers of the Comptroller and Auditor
General over the nationalized industries is misconceived. Such
industries should either be in the market or under ministerial
control.

The parliamentary committees attached to various departments
of government should be retained. I doubt if it would be worth
while in the first year or two of its power or influence for the
Alliance to attempt any dramatic alterations to the procedures
of the Commons. Any such move would provoke long discussions,

which would consume time and energy better taken up by other matters. In the long run the Commons' procedures must be made more businesslike. But the Government itself could greatly assist the dispatch of business by refraining from issuing the spate of Bills, regulations and so on which up to now Governments have released in increasing numbers every session.

Even if changing the structure of Britain's government takes time, a start could be made in the first session of Parliament. I am not convinced of the case for regional authorities in England, but so much discussion has already taken place about the government of Scotland, Wales and Northern Ireland that it should be possible to introduce a Bill in the first session, or at least in the second. Such a Bill must entitle the Parliaments of Scotland, Wales and Northern Ireland to levy certain taxes. It must greatly reduce the representation of these three interests at Westminster. I wrote a pamphlet some years ago, *A Roar for the Lion*, in which I gave my view as to how Scottish self-government should proceed, building from the local foundations upwards. I believe that if it is worth pursuing at all, self-government for Scotland, the Principality and the Province must go a considerable way – indeed, in the case of Scotland, leaving only defence, foreign affairs, the management of the currency and major planning and financial decisions in London.

There will remain an important role for the central government in macro-economic management and in providing temporary assistance to certain industries. As William Rodgers points out in *The Politics of Change*: 'There are two powerful reasons why Governments choose to spend public money on industrial purposes: to mitigate the social consequences of unrestrained market forces and to improve unsatisfactory performance. The principal error in state intervention has been all too often deliberately to confuse these purposes' (p. 84). I agree. I would argue that the first of these purposes should be met by welfare payments. The second is a legitimate but difficult field for public intervention, often achieved by removing obstacles (burdensome taxation, for example).

Even in the short term, the Alliance must bear its ultimate aim in mind. Promises of immediate results should be muted. In the first year or two of government the task will be to permit some increase in demand and to encourage investment. I am not convinced that this will require an incomes policy, but if one is necessary, it should be a crude and temporary one. In these early years steps must be taken at least to simplify taxation and the operation of the social services so that they will be ready to move to a new structure. The Budget should be recast to distinguish capital from revenue and productive from unproductive expenditure.

In the longer term the main task is to reform our financial and industrial organization. The Alliance must either reform the savings banks or introduce new local banking facilities to channel local savings into local investment. It must find some way of isolating the harmful effects of the great sums of money that flow across the Exchanges for no better reason than that they can earn a little more elsewhere. The effects of such movements (for instance, as Governments raise interest rates) can be harmful to industry and commerce, yet they have no connection with changes in industry and commerce. They have no justification in any improvement or decline in the prospects of business. We should examine new methods of handling the currency and the related money and credit supply.

We should, in the short run, undertake a greater volume of public investment in productive industries, such as the new technologies, and in essential services. But at this time of unemployment a main aim must be to remove some of the penalties for employing labour.

Our longer-term industrial policy, in accord with our general outlook, must give high priority to the engagement of employees in the running of industry and services of all kinds. Denationalization policies should encompass co-operatives or management take-overs. The increasingly important service industries, which are often best run by small units and which sometimes require little capital, are well suited to co-operative organization. Those nationalized industries which could be profitable should be hived off. Where possible, they should be broken down into co-operatives of their own workers.

'Industrial relations' must be interpreted more widely than as the relationship of employer and employed. The idea of a divide — on one side of which stand the employers, few in number, fenced about by secrecy and privilege, whose business it is to give orders, on the other side the great mass of the employed whose business is ultimately to obey, like the infantry in battle — is out of date and out of tune. It descends from the time when size was all, when industry was to be organized in bigger and bigger units, in which the only relationships could be those of officers and men in the Victorian army. These large units have proved, in most industries, to be as inefficient as some of us foretold, but the attitudes which accompanied the old veneration of economies of scale linger on. The workers' councils, supervisory boards and consultative councils that are often cited as symbols of the amelioration of the relationship between employers and workers usually still assume that industry will continue to be organized in large units, with a chasm between employers and employed and fairly uniform conditions of work. The Alliance must consider the break-up of such units, so that, for instance, track maintenance and catering might be hived off from the running of railway services. Within each group work-sharing, part-time employment, differing hours of work for men and women and other adjustments to modern life must become more normal. Groups of mutually supportive co-operatives, backed by common banking and accountancy and selling services, will break down the great divide that has established the workers as owners of capital and employers as purveyors of managerial skills.

Services which cannot or should not be subjected to the market — the best economic regulator and the best method of offering choice — should be brought under direct parliamentary (or at least democratic) control. The quango is an organization to be regarded with some suspicion. It is often responsible neither to the market nor to democratic control. It lives on public funds but is usually manned by boards appointed from the old boy network. I do not say that quangos should never be instituted. Some have done good work. But they are hybrids bereft of virility. They relieve Ministers of responsibility for answering criticisms, and they provide a haven for retired friends of the Establishment who wish to supplement their pensions.

As for education, I have suggested that the Alliance should initiate experiments with vouchers for post-secondary education for use by school-leavers, instead of grants, to finance a year in industry, the social services or some other field. Further, we should be prepared to finance postgraduate education through loans.

In foreign affairs I think that we should firmly support NATO and the Western Alliance. We should retain the nuclear deterrent for the Alliance. Whether that would entail indefinitely the main-tenance of a British nuclear deterrent, as opposed to a Western Alliance deterrent, I doubt. We might accept the cruise missiles but not *Trident*.

As for disarmament, this must be multilateral. I regard it as one of the chief virtues of the Alliance that it offers to people who generally regard themselves as being on the left, but reject uni-lateral disarmament, a party which displays a keen sense of urgency about disarmament but is not unilateralist. A study should be undertaken immediately of how far the defence Ministries and the armament industry have developed a momentum of their own. The possibility that the armament interest may over-insure is rendered all the more plausible by the difficulty of making it accountable for the vast sums of money that it handles. More-over, its operations are inevitably wrapped in secrecy.

Over the EEC too there can be no question. The Alliance offers a pro-European party of the liberal left to those who, for other reasons, are not Tories but who believe that we should stay in Europe.

Even if the Alliance is not in a position, after the election, to put the ideas which I advocate into practice, these will, I believe, remain essential if Britain is to pull herself out of her stagnant mood. As I have said, our stagnation is not without its virtues. It is by no means certain that a majority of the British want to bestir themselves. But believing, as I do, that they should bestir them-selves, I also believe that they will require to face changes in many of our institutions, changes which will be strongly opposed by bureaucrats of all kinds. If not the Alliance then some other party must tackle the failure of these institutions to meet our needs.

This short book is about the general philosophy that I would like to see the Alliance adopt, with some indications as to how it might proceed to translate it into legislation. The book is not about the genesis or the organization of the Alliance, nor is it about electoral strategy or tactics. I make no prophecy about the party's success. Nevertheless, I would like to finish by touching on some wider themes.

For the last sixty years Liberals have been swimming against the tide, which, boosted by two world wars, has been flowing in favour of the expansion of the state hand in hand with corporatism. The age has been highly political, in that government — a political creature — has made great inroads into our lives. That has by no means been all to the bad, nor have Liberals always opposed it. On the contrary, government action for the relief of poverty may be said to have started, or to have taken a leap forward, with Mr Asquith's Government. The age has been highly political in another sense as well. Many organizations, local government among them, have sought political roles.

Yet within the last thirty years or so there has been some decline of interest in political philosophy. Discussion about the kind of country we want to construct and the place of individuals in it has given way to psephology, the study of who is going to win elections and why — rather like the study of horse breeding and horse racing. Politics has become not so much a means of achieving some common good as a means by which various interest groups can pursue their own advantage.

It may seem paradoxical that a free, individualist, liberal society can exist only when there are strong bonds to hold it together. Some of these bonds — such as common tradition, respect for generally accepted values, reverence for institutions, restraint upon greed — have weakened. All are essential to liberalism. *Laissez-faire*, a free market, individual choice, tolerance must be practised within the limits imposed by regard for the community. The order imposed by dictatorships takes over when natural order breaks down. The machinery of the state must then enforce some sort of order based on fear, not consent. This has happened all over the world, with disastrous results.

I believe that one of the reasons why this has happened is because a liberal society does not offer many positions of power to ambitious men and women. Countries today produce a great number of educated citizens, few of whom are cut out to satisfy their ambitions in commerce, fewer still prepared to resign themselves to being subordinate. With all their horror, wars release certain pressures built up by peace. They open up advancement in all sorts of directions. When war is not available politics (local, trade union, bureaucratic) are alternative ladders. The 'displacement' by war of which Peacock and Wiseman write in their book *The Growth of Public Expenditure in the United Kingdom* not only provokes a landslide of government expenditure but also displaces and replaces large numbers of office holders and greatly increases the number of offices to be held.

Now we may be entering a less political era. I say 'may' because I am by no means certain. I think, however, that I detect a certain disillusionment with recent political action. Too many so-called reforms have made things worse. The state's incursion into the running of industry and services through the nationalized sector has not proved a success. Many people find that local government offers the ratepayer a poor bargain. But the most serious examples of political failure are Northern Ireland, unemployment and disarmament. It may be unfair to expect national Parliaments to deal with such matters. But the optimism which existed after the war, when Governments pledged themselves to maintain full employment and believed that they could do it, has disappeared. It is apparent that with all the forces at its disposal the state cannot stamp out terrorism in Northern Ireland. Nor do people any longer have faith in such ideas as collective security or the UN, which depend on government action.

It seems to me possible, therefore, that people may look rather more to forms of activity other than the political. This should be encouraging for Liberals. They have always believed in a pluralist society. What they should now be doing is developing the framework for such a society.

I believe that the Liberal Party and the SDP will eventually merge — though not in the immediate future. When I first read the books of David Owen and Bill Rodgers I saw no reason why they should not be members of the Liberal Party. However, for understandable reasons the two parties remain separate, though in alliance. The SDP will continue, I think, to put more emphasis on parliamentary action. The Liberal tradition should develop in parallel, stressing the role of the individual through a variety of communities and institutions. It should also ensure that there are many other methods besides politics by which talented men and women can find satisfaction.

I have throughout this book drawn a distinction between the short and the long term. In the short term the Alliance should muster the support of all those who seek a modification of recent Tory policies. It should display sensitivity to the reactions of those who see not only their livelihood but also cherished and familiar bulwarks like their communities and their professions sacrificed (as they believe) to a cold economic theory. In this they will not differ much from Tory 'wets' or moderate Labour. But in the longer term the Alliance must propound more radical ideas, such as those that I have suggested in this book.

New proposals will also come from other sources. The Tories, indeed, are making the running at present. We should no more be alarmed in the longer term that some of our ideas coincide with some of theirs than we should be ashamed in the short run of going the same way as moderate Labour. The ultimate contribution of the Alliance to British politics may be that it will persuade the British people to accept new ideas. To achieve this it must be receptive to their fears as well as their hopes.

Gradualism is an honourable feature of British history — though sometimes the process of change has been too gradual. We must have a clear idea of the sort of society we want. It may be very different from that of today, but we must carry with us the great middle range of the British, particularly the mass of ordinary work people, convincing them that we offer them a better life, in a more satisfactory society, than state socialism and the bureaucracies can provide.

Select Bibliography

Ball, R. J. *Money and Employment*, London: Macmillan, 1982

Bradley, I., *Breaking the Mould?*, Oxford: Martin Robertson, 1981

Brittan, S., *How to End the Monetarist Controversy*, London: Institute of Economic Affairs, 1982

Bruce-Gardyne, J., and Lawson, N., *The Power Game: An Examination of Decision-Making in Government*, London: Macmillan, 1976

Drucker, P., *The New Society*, London: William Heinemann, 1951

Grimond, J., *The Liberal Future*, London: Faber and Faber, 1959

Grimond, J., *The Liberal Challenge*, London: Hollis, 1963

Grimond, J., *Bureaucratic Blight*, London: Liberal Party Publications Dept., 1966

Grimond, J., *The Common Welfare*, London: Temple Smith, 1978

Haseler, S., *The Tragedy of Labour*, Oxford: Basil Blackwell, 1980

Howard, M., *War and the Liberal Conscience*, London: Temple Smith, 1978

Howard, M., *Weapons and Peace*, London: David Davies Memorial Institute of International Studies, 1983

Lagun-Aro. The Non-Profit Making Social Welfare Mutuality of the Mondragon Co-operatives. A Report Prepared for the Nuffield Foundation. London: Job Ownership Limited, 1982

Le Grand, J., *The Strategy of Equality: Redistribution and the Social Services*, London: Allen and Unwin, 1982

Meade, J. E., *Stagflation*, vol. 1: *Wage-Fixing*, London: Allen and Unwin, 1982

Oakeshott, R., *The Case for Workers' Co-ops*, London: Routledge and Kegan Paul, 1979

Owen, D., *Face the Future*, London: Jonathan Cape, 1981

Peacock, A. T., and Wiseman, J., *The Growth of Public Expenditure in the United Kingdom*, Princeton, NJ: Princeton University Press for the National Bureau of Economic Research, 1966

Plender, J., *That's the Way the Money Goes: The Financial Institutions and the Nation's Savings*, London: André Deutsch, 1982

Popper, K., *The Open Society and its Enemies*, London: Routledge and Kegan Paul, 1945

Rodgers, W., *The Politics of Change*, London: Secker and Warburg, 1982

Rowley, C. K., and Wiseman, J., 'Inflation versus Unemployment: Is the Government Impotent?', *National Westminster Bank Quarterly Review*, February 1983

Seldon, A., *Charge*, London: Temple Smith, 1977

Smith, T., *The Politics of the Corporate Economy*, Oxford: Martin Robertson, 1979

Taverne, D., *The Future of the Left*, London: Jonathan Cape, 1974

Warnock, M., *Education: The Way Ahead*, Oxford: Basil Blackwell/Mainstream Book Club, 1979

Williams, S., *Politics is for People*, Harmondsworth: Penguin, 1981

Young, M., and Hall, P., *The Middle of the Night*, Pamphlet No. 4, Tawney Society, 1982

Index

Alliance:
  aims, long-term, 1−2, 26−8, 51, 65,
    76, 83, 85, 86−105, 160, 165−6,
    168
  aims, short-term, 1, 65−85, 161−3,
    168
  corporatism, 46−7
  defence policy, 24, 155−7, 165
  devolution, 54−6
  educational policies, 126, 128−9,
    131−5, 164−5
  foreign policy, 152−4, 165
  law and order, 142
  leadership, 6, 29
  policies proposed, 27- 31, 57−8, 61
  and welfare services, 110, 112,
    117−18, 120−1, 124
  see also economy; incomes policy;
    industrial relations; inflation
Amory, Derek Heathcote, 14
Arismende, Father, 95
Asquith, H. H., 59, 166

Ball, R. J., 77−8
Bank of England, 18, 104
Beveridge, William, 2−3, 4, 10, 113−14,
  116
Bologna, social services scheme, 123−4
Boyson, Rhodes, 126−7
Brittan, Samuel, 24, 71−2
Buckingham, University of, 131
Budget, recasting of, 82−3, 163
bureaucracy, state, 6, 50, 109−10, 165,
  168
  development of, 3−4, 7−8

expansion of, 2, 10−12, 14, 23, 30,
  44−5, 153
and expectations, 86−8
in nationalized industries, 92
relation with Ministers, 51
see also industry; local government
Burke, Edmund, 62
Burnet, Alastair, 12
businesses, small, 14−15
  and expectations, 86−7
  incentives for, 17, 21, 82, 92, 100
Butler, R. A., 13−14
'Butsekllism', 10−11

Caldecote, Lord, 85
capitalism, state, 90
centralization:
  in economic planning, 78, 84- 5
  effects of, 3−5, 8, 71−2
  financial system, 102−4
  in media, 12−13
  in welfare services, 35−6
  see also decentralization
Chamberlain, Neville, 149
child benefit, proposed increase in, 65
choice, individual:
  and education, 126, 127, 134
  extension of, 99, 109−11, 118−19,
    166
  limitation of, 8
Churchill, Winston, 68
City of London, and industrial finance,
  17−18, 19, 80, 103−4
Civil Service, 3, 14, 57, 133−4
  as economic interest, 7, 86- 7

reduction in, 20
relation with Ministers, 51, 68
closed shop:
    legal profession, 142
    and trade unions, 101
Commonwealth, policy towards, 147
communism:
    economy of, 90
    relations with, 148–51
    threat of, 21, 22–3, 24
community politics, 2, 4–5, 25, 35, 39,
    111, 160–1, 167–8
    community management of welfare
        services, 120, 122–5
    and individual achievement, 116
competition in industry, encouragement
    of, 92–3, 99
    capital and labour, 93
    lack of, in nationalized industries, 3, 9,
        20
Confederation of British Industries (CBI),
    47–8, 87
Conservative Party:
    economic policy, 16–17, 18–21, 26,
        87
    political reform, 51
    see also nationalized industries
constitution, written, need for, 62
consumer, needs of, 43, 90, 91, 105
co-operatives, 3, 24, 37, 92, 101
    consumers', 94
    housing, 39, 83–4
    no support for, 19
    policies, for, 28, 29, 83, 85, 93–6,
        105, 163
    in public industries, 96–7, 163–4
    in social services provision, 39, 121–4
corporatism, 45–9, 166
cruise missiles, 156, 165

Day, Robin, 12
decentralization, 133, 140, 160
    of financial system, 103–5
    of government, 6, 28, 54–6
    of nationalized industries, 3, 83
    of welfare services, 5–6, 124
    see also centralization
defence policy, aims of, 147–50, 155–9
    conventional forces, 24, 157
    see also disarmament; nuclear weapons

demand:
    level of, 70
    management of, 20–1, 66–7, 69–70,
        84, 162
deterrence, policy of, 24, 29, 149–51,
    155–9, 165
development:
    agencies, 73, 84–5
    and local authority provisions, 38–9,
        73
Devlin, Lord, 138
devolution, 29, 54
differentials, traditional, 19, 90
disarmament:
    multilateral, 156–7, 159, 165, 167
    unilateral, 51, 155–6, 157–8
Drucker, Peter, 117

economy:
    Alliance proposals for, 65–6, 69
    demand management, 66–7, 69–70, 84
    growth in, 10, 16, 69–70, 77, 88–9
    management of, 2–3, 5–6, 9–10, 90
    reform in, 20, 75–7
    supply management, 70–4, 79, 82–3
    see also Conservative Party; Labour
        party; monetarism
economy, mixed, 6, 27–30
Eden, Douglas, 110, 121
education, 22, 126–35
    and bureaucracy, 11, 109
    comprehensive, 127
    content of, 127–8
    finance for, 37, 117, 128, 131–2, 134
    and income level, 5, 115, 134–5
    loans, 132, 135, 165
    Ministry of, need for, 128
    and needs of local community, 36, 37
        128
    practical training, 129–31
    primary, 126
    private, 110, 128–9, 134
    school-leaving age, 129, 138
    tertiary, 37, 129–32, 135
    voucher systems, 126, 129–31, 134,
        164–6
    see also morality; universities
employment:
    measures to increase, 65–6, 69–71,
        75, 78–9, 82–4

removal of taxation on, 69, 163
energy, high costs of, 18, 20, 66
entrepreneur:
   disregard of, 2–3, 17, 21
   encouragement for, 73, 99–101
Equity Capital for Industry, 17
European Economic Community (EEC):
   commitment to, 29, 82, 147, 151–2, 165
   control of expenditure, 152–3
   control of regulations, 153
   regional aid, 89, 153
exchange rate, 65, 80
expectations, 66, 86–90
expenditure, government:
   and EEC, 152–3
   and expectations, 87–8
   increase in, 16, 43–4, 48, 65–6, 69, 74, 112, 167
   and investment, 66–8, 71–3, 82–3
   and production, 43–4, 45–6, 83, 163
   restrictions in, 44–5
   and revenue, 50, 61
   scrutiny of, 60, 161

foreign policy, 147–54, 165
   Commonwealth, 147
   overseas aid, 153–4
   United Nations, 147–8
   USSR, 147–51
   and world prosperity, 151
   see also EEC; trade, international
Friedman, Milton, 66

Gaitskell, Hugh, 6, 8
Gorer, Geoffrey, 137
government, central, 2–3, 9, 43–62, 119, 160–1, 166
   areas of concern, 35, 162
   Commons business arrangements, 61–2, 161–2
   Conservative policies, 18, 27
   and economic growth, 69–70, 90–1
   and expectations, 22, 86–8
   and the general interest, 48–9, 58–60
   increases in, 16, 43, 167
   and institutions, 45–8, 52, 57
   reconsideration necessary, 16, 26–7, 51, 60, 91–2, 94, 109–10, 161

   as remote from electorate, 50–1, 52–3, 58, 61–2
   specialist committees, 21, 45, 60–1, 161
   see also economy, management of; expenditure, government; reform, political; Scotland; Wales; welfare services
Grossart, Michael, 102
growth, economic, 77, 88–9
   decline in, 10, 16, 90–1

Harris of High Cross, Lord (Ralph), 24, 43
Haseler, Stephen, 110, 121
Hayek, F. A., 24
Healey, Denis, 66
health service:
   and bureaucracy, 11
   finance for, 117–18, 134
   and income level, 5, 115, 120
   insurance voucher scheme, 118–20, 161
   private medicine, 120
Highlands and Islands Development Board, 39, 73, 84–5, 102, 104
Hitler, Adolf, 23
Hobbes, Thomas, 74
Holt, Arthur, 20
Hordern, Peter, 128
House of Lords:
   abolition of, 16
   as corporate chamber, 47–8
   reform of, 49, 58–60, 62
housing, 84
   co-operatives, 39, 83–4
   and crime, 137
   financing of, 117–18, 120–1
   and income level, 115
   local authority provision, 39–40, 120
   mortgage relief, reduction of, 115, 121
   owner-occupied, 83
   private sector, 120–1
   public investment in, 39, 83–4, 118
Howard, Michael, 150
Howe, Geoffrey, 20, 69
Hunt, Lord Crowther (Norman), 70, 134

incomes:
  high, 75—6
  minimum, 38, 47, 113—14, 117—18,
    120, 135, 160
incomes policy, 82
  Alliance proposals, 29, 65, 73- 7, 88
  long-term, 73—4, 76—80, 99
  public-sector, 76
  short-term, 75—6, 163
individual, attitudes towards, 8, 23, 27—9,
    92, 111, 116, 126, 134, 160, 166,
    168
  and corporatism, 46—8
  and crime, 139—40
Industrial and Commercial Finance
    Corporation (ICFC), 17, 73, 85, 102
industrial relations, 143
  Alliance policies, 76, 92, 105, 163—4
  Conservative policies, 19, 21
  poor state of, 15
industry:
  bureaucracy in, 17, 92, 100
  effects of monetarism, 19—20
  lack of efficiency, 14, 19
  management of, 98—100
  ownership of, 35, 76, 83, 85, 93—5,
    105, 163
  reform in structure, 27, 30, 47, 80—1,
    91—101
  regional, decline in, 14
  protection of, 80—2
  see also co-operatives; investment;
    nationalized industries; worker
    participation
inflation:
  Alliance policies, 29, 69, 73, 75, 80
  increase in, 15, 16—17, 20, 65—7, 89
  reduction in, 20, 87
  and unemployment, 17, 26, 65, 74, 82
  wage-based, 75
insurance funds, effects on investment,
    68, 103—4
interest rates, high level of, 19—20, 80
investment, 162
  decline in, 71—2
  in industry, 18, 81, 83—5, 101—4,
    163
  local, 71, 73, 84, 102, 104—5, 163
  overseas, 89, 103
  public-sector, 9, 20, 66—8, 73, 83

Japan, industrial organization in, 98—9,
    105
Jenkins Roy, 1, 6, 29, 66, 69, 73, 88,
    152

Kee, Robert, 12
Kennedy, Ludovic, 12
Keynes, J. M., 2—3, 29, 46, 74, 83
Keynesianism, *versus* monetarism,
    66—8

Labour Party, 26—7
  economic policy, 16—17
  and political reform, 51
  and state socialism, 3, 6, 26
  and trade unions, 16, 26
Lagun-Aro, 121—3
Law, Richard, 60
law and order, 136—43, 166
  and community police, 139—42
  and education, 140, 143
  historical background, 136—7
  increase in crime, 137—8
  legal system, 142
Layard, Richard, 71, 77—8
le Grand, Julian, 114—17, 119
Liberal Party:
  community politics, 25, 27
  leadership, 24—5, 27—8, 77
  in local government, 25, 110—11
  policies of, 1, 24—31, 72—3, 77, 92,
    166—8
  regional councils, 54
local government, 5—6, 35—42
  and bureaucracy, 11, 17, 35—6
  expansion of intersets, 11—12, 20, 38,
    166—7
  finance for, 35—7, 39, 40—1, 161
  and law and order, 143
  planning, 40
  polarization in, 36
  powers of, 37—40, 161
  and pressure groups, 50
  and provision of social services, 39
  reform, 1972, 11, 17, 55
  see also development; education;
    housing; transport

Macmillan, Harold, 13—14
Macrae, Norman, 24, 97, 105

management:
  of nationalized industries, 38
  take-overs of nationalized industries,
    19, 21, 85, 97, 163
market, free, 22, 35, 56—7, 71, 74, 91—2,
    104, 166
  control of market forces, 3
Meade, J.E., 78—9, 82
media, influence of, 8, 12—13, 50, 139
Mondragon, co-operatives at, 94—6, 101,
    105, 121
monetarism, 1, 26, 46, 74
  effects of, 19—20, 65
  see also Keynesianism
monopolies:
  legislation on, 91
  private industrial, 3
  state, 3, 6—7, 9, 20, 38, 90, 92
morality:
  and education, 127, 130, 140
  and institutions, 46
  and law, 137—40
  need for, 29, 74
  uncertainty about, 8, 11, 21, 22—3
  of war, 157—8
Murray, John, 81—2

National Insurance surcharge, 65, 71
nationalized industries, 14, 90, 92, 161,
    163, 167
  and Alliance policies, 29
  Conservative policies, 17, 19—21, 27
  co-operatives in, 96—7
  efficiency of, 8—10, 38
  and expectations, 87
  investment in, 20, 83—5
  and Labour Government, 3, 6
  wage levels in, 78
  see also monopolies, state; privatization
NATO, 29, 147, 155, 158, 165
Noble, Iain, 102
Northern Ireland:
  and EEC intervention, 152
  government of, 56, 162
  political failure in, 167
nuclear weapons, policy on, 24, 29,
    149—50, 155—9, 165

Oakeshott, Robert, 24, 121—3
Owen, David, 6, 29, 77, 119, 120—1, 167

Paish, Frank, 72
Peacock, Alan, 24, 44, 70, 167
pension funds, effect on investment,
    17—19, 68, 103—4
pensioners, earnings rule abolition pro-
    posed, 65
pensions, indexed, 14, 19, 44, 76
  and expectations, 86—7
planning:
  central, 40
  local, 40, 143
Plender, John, 68, 102—3
Polavis, 156
police, 139—42
poverty, 4, 28, 166
  and crime, 137
  European, 89, 92, 153
  worldwide, 21—3
pressure groups, 43—5, 48—9, 50, 59
prices:
  control of, 74
  freeze on, 76
  rises, 15, 22, 88
  stability, 77
privatization of nationalized industries,
    89, 97
production:
  incentives for, 70—1
  levels of, 20, 22, 70, 74, 80, 83
Profumo, J. 145
protection, 80—2
public good:
  education as, 37, 135
  and health care, 118, 120
  local authority responsibilities, 37
public sector borrowing requirement
    (PSBR), 80, 83
  proposed level, 65, 69, 72—3, 85

quangos, 7, 16, 20, 43, 164

rates, 11, 40—2
referenda, necessity for, 59—60
reform, political, 20—1, 27, 44, 48—50,
    51, 76
  'added Members', 58
  abolition of trade union sponsorship,
    49
  electoral reform, 52—60, 62
  single-Member constituencies, 52,
    58, 59

single transferable vote, 53, 57, 59
  see also Northern Ireland; Scotland;
    Wales
regional councils, Alliance proposals,
    29, 54
regions:
  assistance for, 3, 71−2, 153
  disregard for, 17
Rhys-Williams, Brandon, 113
Rhys-Williams, Lady, 113
riots, racial, 143
Rodgers, William, 6, 29−30, 162, 167

Scarman, Lord, 143
Scotland:
  less representation at Westminster, 55
  self-government, 29, 54−7, 59, 162
Seebohm, Lord, 85
Seldon, Arthur, 24, 114, 117, 118−19, 126
Social Democratic Party, 1, 6, 26, 49, 51,
    73, 87−8, 167−8
  defence policies, 156
  on education, 128−9, 133
  policies, 29−30, 77−8, 80−1, 112,
    120−1, 124
  regional government, 54
  see also Alliance
socialism, non-state, 28−9, 101, 160
socialism, state, 3, 6, 25−6, 92−3, 168
  and economic growth, 10, 90−1
  effects of, 16, 30, 119
Stalin, Joseph, 23
Steel, David, 26, 29
Suez crisis, effects of, 13−14
supply:
  increase in money supply, 17, 19−20,
    65−6, 73−4, 79, 80, 82
  management of, 70−4

Taverne, Dick, 112
tax/benefit system, Alliance proposals,
    65, 112−13
taxation, 44, 67, 152−3
  complexity of, 15, 21, 82, 92, 163
  cuts in, 82
  on employment, 69, 71−2
  income tax, local, 41−2
  indirect, 41−2
  local, 40−2, 161
  Parliamentary scrutiny of, 60

percentage tax, 41−2
reverse income tax, 113−14, 117
  on wage increases, 77
  see also Value Added Tax
teacher training, 128
technologies, new, 67, 70, 88−9, 97
Thatcher, Margaret, 52, 66
Thorpe, Jeremy, 25−6
trade, international:
  British dependence on, 16, 21, 147, 151
  and protectionism, 80−2
  and world prosperity, 70, 89, 151
trade unions, 67−8
  Alliance policies, 29−30, 74
  and decentralization, 6
  and efficiency of industry, 14, 101
  and expectations, 86
  influence on Labour Party, 6, 16, 26
  representation in Parliament, 47−8
  sponsorship of MPs, 48−9
  and state socialism, 16, 26
  and wage demands, 66, 74, 77, 79, 101
  see also closed shop
transport:
  costs of, 117−18
  and income level, 116
  provision of by local authority, 38
  public investment, 83, 118, 161
Treasury:
  and general interest, 49
  out of touch with industry, 14−15, 18
Trident 156, 165

unemployment, 66, 84
  and crime, 138
  increase in, 15, 17, 20, 26, 74, 167
  policies for reduction in, 65, 69−72
uniformity, rejection of, 5−6, 35−6, 37
United Nations, policy towards, 147−8, 167
universities, 46, 47, 130−4, 135, 140
University Grants Committee (UGC), 132
USA, 14
  and defence policies, 155−6
USSR/threat from, 23−4, 147−51, 155−9

Value Added Tax (VAT), 18, 65, 66

wages:
  high levels of, 15, 18−19, 20, 21−2,
    66, 76, 99, 101

restriction on, 73—6, 77—8, 87—8
see also incomes policy
Wales, self-government for, 29, 54—7, 59, 162
Walker, Peter, 84
Walker, Ronald, 93
war, threat of, 21, 24, 147—51, 153, 155—6, 158—9
Warnock, Mary, 127—8
wealth:
   generation of, 3, 109, 111
   redistribution of, 2, 5, 114
welfare services, 109—25, 138, 160
   and bureaucracy, 11, 26, 76, 82, 109—10, 117, 122, 124—5
   community management, 120, 122—5
   co-operatives proposed, 39, 121—4, 160

decline in, 39
and equality of opportunity, 114—17
and expectations, 87, 109—10
local authority provision, 39, 110—11, 160
provision of, 3, 4—5, 110—12
reform of, 27, 30, 117—21, 124—5, 163
and taxation, 10, 112—13
voluntary provision, 125
Williams, Shirley, 6, 29, 110, 125, 132—3
Wilson, Harold, 14, 15
Wiseman, Jack, 44, 167
worker participation, 19, 35, 83, 94, 97
   in social services provision, 121—2

Young, Michael (Lord Young of Dartington), 121, 123